Handel's Messiah

FROM SCRATCH®

Tenor edition

First published in 2002 by

Artemis | EDITIONS

an imprint of Artemis Music Limited
Pinewood Studios
Pinewood Road
Iver Heath
Buckinghamshire
SL0 0NH

Order No: ART00003
ISBN: 1-904411-02-9
ISMN: M 57025 002 8

Project editor: James Sleigh
Producer: Mike Sheppard
Engineer: Martin Atkinson
Music setting: Jackie Leigh
Cover design: Ripe

Cover image: 'Christ Painting Near Telephone' by Joel Simon, courtesy of Getty Images
Printed in the United Kingdom by Halstan & Co. Ltd.
Recorded at Phoenix Studios, London and M.A.R.S. Studios

The Artemis Chorus & Sinfonia

Conductor:	David Meacock
Women:	Jacqeline Barron, Julia Batchelor, Helen Foster Brookes, Heather Cairncross, Suzanne Flowers, Eleanor Meynell, Jenny O'Grady, Alison Pace, Kim Porter, Olive Simpson, Rachel Weston, Karen Woodhouse
Men:	Patrick Ardagh-Walter, Paul Badley, Christopher Dee, Robert Fardell, Graham Godfrey, Simon Grant, Edward Hands, Gerald Place, David Porter-Thomas, Jonathan Rathbone, Richard Weston
Leader:	Michael Davis
1st violins:	John Georgiadis, Adrian Levine, Clive Lander, Maciej Rakowski, John Bradbury
2nd violins:	Peter Benson, Pan Hon Lee, David Ogden, Howard Ball, Roger Garland, David Randall
Violas:	Rusen Gunes, George Robertson, Stephen Shakeshaft, Cathryn McCraken
'Cellos:	Anthony Pleeth, David Bucknall, David Daniels, Paul Kegg
Double Bass:	Allen Walley, Lynda Houghton
Oboes:	John Anderson, Christopher O'Neal
Trumpets:	Crispian Steele-Perkins, Joe Atkins
Bassoon:	Gavin McNaughton
Harpsichord:	Leslie Pearson
Percussion:	John Gregory Knowles

About the editor

David Meacock studied piano with Iris du Prè (mother of the famous 'cellist) and then Eric Hope K.T., a pupil of Solomon. After studying piano (with Kendall Taylor CBE) and conducting at the Royal College of Music (where, in his first term, David sang in the choir under Sir David Willcocks), David completed a Masters degree at Reading University. More recently, he participated in a Michael Tilson Thomas led International Conductors' Masterclass in USA.

In 1992, David formed what was to become the fully professional A40 Concert Orchestra and, after conducting Great Missenden Choral Society for five years, he formed the Beaconsfield-based A40 Choir in 1995. Apart from its regular local performances, the choir has broadcast on Classic FM and has twice sung in the Queen Elizabeth Hall as well as appearing in Rouen cathedral. They have also premièred David's reduced orchestrations of Verdi's *Requiem* and Elgar's *The Dream of Gerontius*, which were specifically designed to make performance of these works possible in smaller venues. Meanwhile, David's début recital at St John's, Smith Square, London, included the Liszt *Sonata*.

David also regularly conducts choral workshops for Concerts From Scratch®, most recently on the Brahms and Mozart *Requiems*.

www.davidmeacock.com

Contents

The Handel House Museum

This edition was produced with the support of the Handel House Museum.

Handel lived at 25 Brook Street, Mayfair, London, for 36 years. It is here that he composed *Messiah* and many of his other greatest works. The house has now been opened as the Handel House Museum with immaculately restored interiors and portraits of Handel and his contemporaries. Live performances in Handel's own rehearsal room bring back to life this landmark in the history of music.

The Handel House Museum, 25 Brook Street, London W1K 4HB.
020 7495 1685

www.handelhouse.org

Messiah From Scratch®

A brief history

Messiah From Scratch® was started by Don Monro and others as a result of sudden inspiration in 1974 and since then has grown into a worldwide phenomenon. Don has subsequently managed all the events, jointly with his wife Ann since 1992.

Sir David Willcocks was first invited to conduct the annual *Messiah From Scratch®* concert in 1976 when the original conductor was away on a sabbatical. He has now conducted *Messiah* every year since, as well as almost every other *From Scratch®* concert at the Royal Albert Hall, London – in total over 70 concerts.

From Scratch® performances have become a national institution and an international phenomenon, with performances taking place all over the world. Such performances have included many other great choral works. The annual *Messiah From Scratch®* performance at the Royal Albert Hall now attracts over 3,000 amateur singers and is one of the world's largest mass participation choral events.

Regular overseas trips are also organised, with enthusiasts travelling to venues such as Halle, Leipzig and Venice to perform music by Handel, J. S. Bach and Vivaldi respectively. Future plans include concerts of music by Beethoven and Schubert in Vienna, and Mozart in Salzburg.

Sir David writes:

'I welcome this new edition of Handel's Messiah, *which is aimed at those singers who wish to supplement the experience that they have gained at organised choral rehearsals with their own private study. Such additional study should enable them to participate in performances of Handel's* Messiah *with improved technique, increased confidence and therefore enhanced enjoyment.'*

An introduction to Handel's *Messiah*

Given that Handel recycled many of his 'greatest hits' when writing *Messiah*, it is hardly surprising that it is his most popular work – and indeed, probably the most performed of the whole choral repertoire.

Messiah was written to raise funds for charitable institutions in Dublin – where it was first performed on 13 April 1742 – so the popularist approach is entirely understandable. A variety of people attended the event, not necessarily to hear an adopted English composer, but rather to support the charities, so Handel needed to appeal to a wide audience.

Ever since its first English performance in 1743, *Messiah* has also been a favourite with choral societies of all sizes, not least because of its modest orchestral forces. It is scored for 2 Oboes, 1 Bassoon, 2 Trumpets, Timpani, Continuo (harpsichord or organ) and Strings. Nowadays, it is often just accompanied by the organ, but in the early 19th Century, newly invented vocal scores were designed for performances with piano accompaniment.

A rehearsal and performance edition

The overwhelming amount of the black ink in a traditional vocal score is irrelevant to the amateur choral singer with limited formal musical training.

This publication has been designed above all as a practical edition, with the needs of the amateur singer the main priority. It is not intended to be an academic treatise – that has already been covered in great detail in many of the other widely available editions. Hence, you will find that the music for arias and recitatives has been omitted, replaced by the text of those items and short cues where they are relevant. Your vocal part is reproduced on a larger stave, with instrumental cues included only where they are helpful. This edition also includes many note-finding tips and strategies that experienced singers use instinctively.

How to use the CDs

Inside the cover of this edition you will also find two CDs. CD1 contains a professional recording of every chorus, performed by the Artemis Chorus & Sinfonia, a group specially assembled for this project, featuring top quality singers and orchestral players from the UK's best professional choirs and orchestras. Your part has been increased in volume by 5db – this should be loud enough for you to pick out your part clearly, but not so loud that it disturbs the overall balance of the recording. The ultimate effect should be the same as if you were standing in the middle of your section of the choir.

CD2 contains vocal warm-ups, tips and exercises to help you prepare for performance, and should be used in conjunction with the detailed notes on each chorus that follow this introduction. The examples are intended to be performed at whatever octave is most comfortable for your voice, as would happen in a choral rehearsal. The relevant track numbers of each CD are indicated at the start of each chorus.

As often happens in a real choir rehearsal, the main themes can be learnt by singing the figure as it first appears, at whatever pitch is convenient, with the expectation that everyone can then apply what has been learnt to their own parts. While a difficult new passage is being learnt, save your voice by taking it down an octave if necessary.

Many of the example passages have been lifted directly from CD1, and the soprano and alto parts have been favoured wherever possible, as they tend to be easier for all voices to follow. The simplified exercises are by the editor and are intended not as a bravura vocal performance, but rather as something that most amateur singers will be able to relate to!

The 'Artemis' performance

The performance tempi on CD1 are deliberately middle-of-the-road – it is quite possible that the speeds chosen by your choir's conductor may be faster or slower, but they are unlikely to be drastically different. Some of the faster choruses are deliberately on the slower side of the tempo scale to aid learning.

In this performance, special attention has been paid to articulation – for example certain notes, usually at the ends of phrases, have been shortened by a quaver to tail the phrase off or to maintain the clarity of changing harmonies. These shortened notes are indicated in the score above each part, but of course you should also watch your conductor carefully for such cut-offs.

In Baroque times double-dotted rhythms were not notated, but are generally expected in a modern performance. The notation in this edition is compatible with generally accepted practice, with other variants shown in small notes. You will need to clarify which your conductor requires. Remember that because of the imprecise nature of music notation, nobody can claim that one way is the only correct way – indeed even Handel himself was prone to change his mind from performance to performance.

Using a soft lead (HB or softer) pencil, lightly note your conductor's instructions, since the next time you sing it, you might have a different conductor with different ideas! Even experienced professional musicians write in their music.

Integrating with other editions

Handel's *Messiah From Scratch®* has been carefully designed to be compatible with the three major existing editions of *Messiah* – Prout, Watkins Shaw, and Edition Peters.

If your conductor is using one of these editions, you will still be able to sing from this book. Page numbers from each edition are clearly marked in this score by the following icons:

Prout: P   Watkins Shaw: WS

Edition Peters: EP

Rehearsal letters are common to nearly all editions, but where variations do occur they are indicated in a similar way.

Practical performance information

Cuts

For many years various numbers have been omitted to shoehorn *Messiah* into the conventional concert length. You need to check with your conductor/concert organiser to see whether there are any cuts and if so, what they are, since your precious time would be better spent preparing choruses which are actually going to be performed!

Choruses 35 and 51 are frequently cut, and in *Messiah From Scratch®* concerts, choruses 21, 37, 39, and 41 are also usually omitted.

Sits and stands

Choirs will normally stand at the beginning of each chorus and sit at the end. Exceptions are all indicated within this edition. Cuts may well require alterations which will normally be given to you by the conductor/concert organiser.

When you have nothing to sing for a short time, count the rests and/or follow the other vocal part or cues until your next entry. Counting will help you enter at the right time, follow other parts, and more easily find your place if you get lost. The note-finding arrows will help you find the correct note when the time comes for your entry.

A guide for quick preparation

It seems that we never have as much time to prepare for a performance as we might ideally like! If you find yourself in this situation, firstly, read through the paragraphs below, and then work through the choruses in the order suggested (omitting any that have been cut, of course), rehearsing with the exercises on CD2, before moving on to singing along with the complete performances on CD1.

The two basic elements of music

Music consists of pitches within time – mastery of these two elements is the key to successful preparation. Always separate the rehearsal of a difficult passage into two tasks: firstly saying the words in rhythm; and secondly, humming or singing the melody to 'la'. When you have mastered these tasks separately, try putting the passage back together again. This is rather like a pianist practising hands separately, or a tennis player learning various shots individually before trying to play a match.

If you are short of preparation time, avoid singing through long passages of easier material – this is a waste of time. Rather, concentrate on the difficult passages, taking half bar lengths at a time and aiming to repeat them four times correctly. This is the approach taken on CD2. It is better to repeat and learn one difficult half bar than spend the same time singing through a complete page only to 'trip up' consistently over that same difficult section – and never master it .

When the two basic elements of music have been mastered, thought can be devoted to the third: intensity – from the quietest *pianissimo* to the most thunderous *fortissimo*.

The following list prioritises contrapuntal (or fugue-type) choruses, where the voices are singing in lines, rather than in chords, and also takes into consideration the overall difficulty (trickier choruses appear towards the top of the list and easier ones towards the end). 'Behold The Lamb Of God' has been put first because mastery of its dotted rhythms will give a good grounding for all other such rhythms throughout the work.

Preparation priority order:

22, 4, 7, 12, 25, 26, 21*, 53a, 53b, 28, 35*, 37*, 41*, 51*, 39*, 17, 9, 24, 33, 46, 44.

* Normally cut from *Messiah From Scratch*® performances

Notation explained

This edition uses the following symbols – often added by experienced choristers to their own parts.

Where the beat might be difficult to follow or where it is important to feel the beat even if you are not singing a new note, it is indicated by a long vertical line.

An upward or downward pointing arrow indicates that the note is higher or lower than might be otherwise instinctively expected (perhaps through a main thematic figure or established pattern being varied).

Cue notes above the stave (♪𝄾) show possible variations (depending on your conductor's personal interpretation) from the norm.

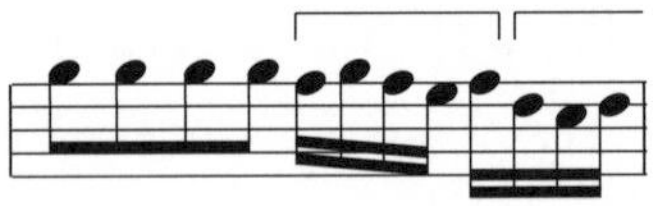

Square brackets indicate repeated patterns underlying long strings of notes. Passages can often be made easier by thinking of them in groups which start and finish at large leaps, rather than in the groups most obvious to the listener.

Note-finding

Note-finding cues are shown wherever they might be helpful – the dotted arrow points from the note that you need to listen for, to your note: +3

The number next to your note shows you the interval between the two, as follows:

= shows that your note is the same, though perhaps at a different octave to the cue note.

+2 indicates an upward interval of a 2nd between the cue note and your note. Similarly, -5 indicates a downward interval of a fifth.

Wherever possible cue notes are taken from the upper parts, as these tend to be heard more easily. Sometimes, the note you need to remember will be one from within your own part.

Warm-ups and teaching hints

Warming up

The voice needs gentle warming up to maximise efficiency and avoid over-tiring, just as with any other muscular or athletic activity. Begin practice sessions with a selection from Tracks 1-18 of CD2, before moving on to the specific exercises from each chorus.

The key to successful singing is natural posture and breathing efficiency. Stand 'high' and poised – not stiffly like the caricature of a Sergeant Major standing to attention. Focus on maximising the distance between the front of both shoulders, and the distance between the shoulders and hips, pushing the crown of the head upwards. If you are sitting, sit ON, rather than IN the chair.

When inhaling, your shoulders should hardly move at all and you should feel the rib cage expand, the stomach moving OUT (not in) and slightly downwards. If you put your hand on your hips, just below the ribcage, you should feel your torso expand as you inhale, coming back in as you exhale. If you have not breathed in this manner before, take it easy as it can initially cause a feeling of dizziness.

Breathe at rests, commas in the text, or as otherwise directed by the conductor. If you need to take an illicit extra breath, you can avoid being noticed by breathing during a vowel and simply rejoining.

Depth of breathing

Here are a couple of exercises that will help you improve your depth of breathing:

1. Keeping the throat open throughout, take six seconds to inhale. Hold for six seconds and then breathe out for six seconds. Don't breathe at all for six seconds, and then start the process again. With practice you will be able to repeat the exercise many times, and you will find that you start to breathe more deeply generally. If you have a regular walk – perhaps to and from a station or bus stop – count six steps for each part of the process.

2. Take a deep breath, and count aloud (one count per second) in your normal talking voice and see how high you can count up to. Now breathe in, and then breathe fully out, and (on an empty tank) start counting. The first time you do this, you will notice that you only achieve a few extra counts on your full lung capacity, but, over time, you will start to notice the difference.

Practising these exercises will improve economy of air usage, ultimately allowing you to control long phrases.

Producing sound

Place the tip of your index finger against your upper palette, with the nail against the back edge of your upper front teeth. Open the mouth gently, so that the tips of your bottom teeth are against the inner fold of the first finger joint (nearest the tip).

Keeping the tongue flat, take a full breath, and sing a G to 'ah'.

CD 2: Track 1

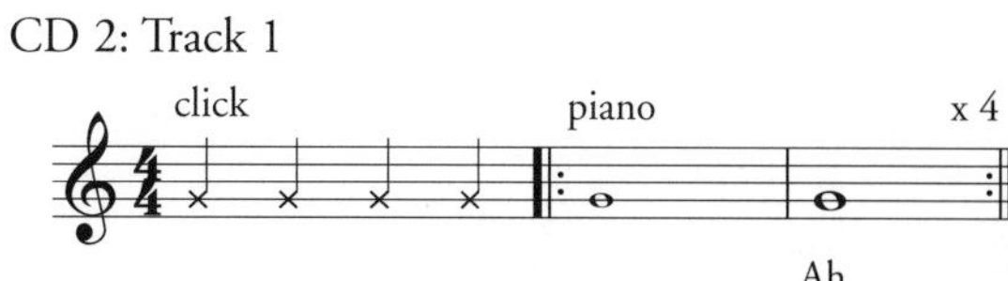

Now *glissando* (slide) slowly, down to a C and back to the starting note, G.

CD 2: Track 2

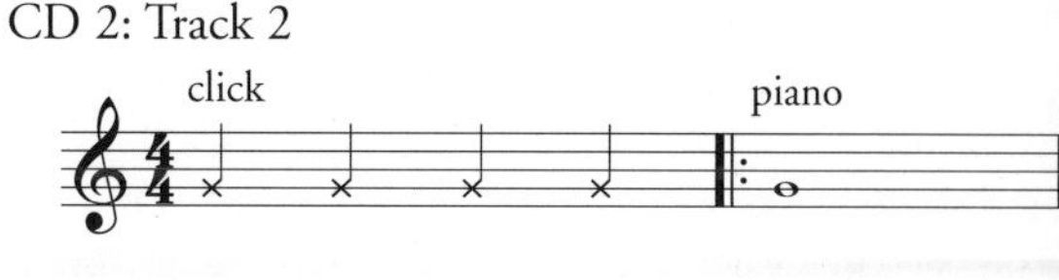

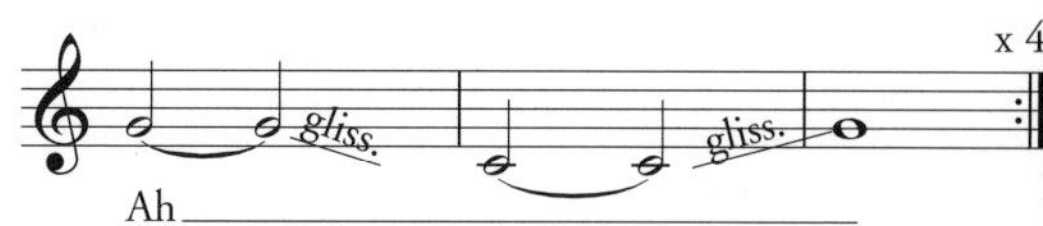

Next, slowly *glissando* up from the lower C to the upper C and back to the lower C.

CD 2: Track 3

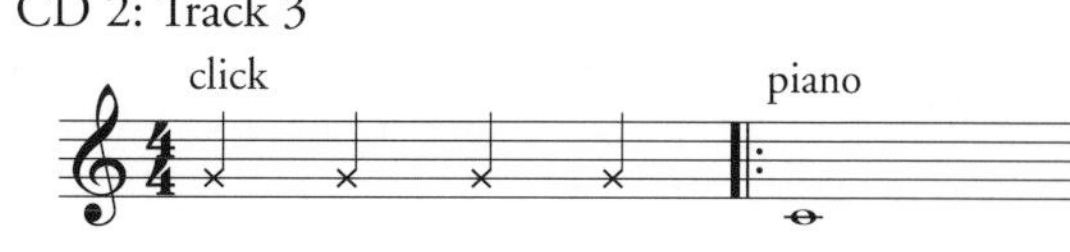

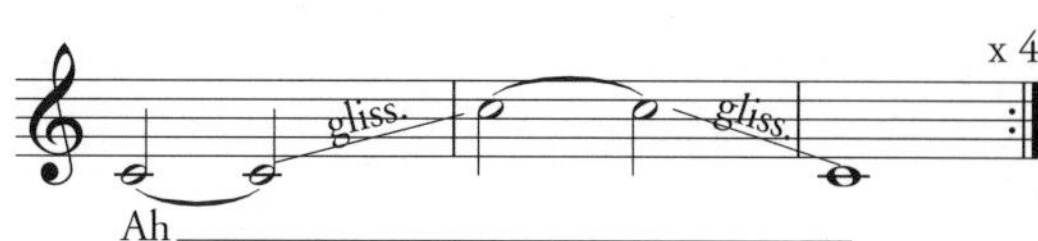

The only thing that affects pitch is your vocal cords, so your head and mouth should remain still throughout.

All of the exercises above can also be practised to a rolled 'r', which prevents you from tightening your throat.

CD 2: Track 4

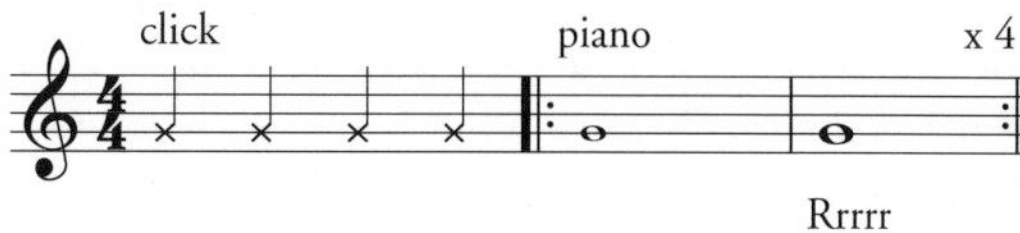

Make sure you also try this along with Tracks 2 & 3.

Another way to optimise your voice is to hum. Beware of clenching your teeth – they should be the same distance apart as previously described, so that the lips are brought gently together over the open teeth. While humming a long note, rotate the lower jaw relative to the upper teeth and the sound will appear to drift in and out of focus. At the point where the sound seems most rounded, or in focus, stop the rotation, and then after a short time open the lips to sing 'ah'.

The singer's secret weapon

Singing for any length of time can cause the vocal cords to become dehydrated. Regular sips of water during a really long singing session – preferably not in sight of a concert audience – will help your voice sound fresh for longer.

Avoid even one unit of alcohol (e.g. one glass of wine or half a pint of beer) within the hour prior to rehearsals or concerts. Firstly, the warm sensation in your throat is in fact the alcohol drying the vocal cords, and secondly your conductor, fellow singers, and your audience all need you to be razor sharp to produce your best. Caffeine-based drinks are also best avoided.

Five basic sounds

Good singing is often described as being based on five Italian vowels, which in turn can be simplified to three: 'ah', 'ee' and 'oo'.

Checking in a mirror, and using the index finger as a guide as above, sing 'ah' – then raise the middle of the tongue to touch the upper palette and some upper teeth to make the vowel 'ee'.

Not surprisingly, 'ee' is sometimes called a *tongue vowel*. To accentuate the difference between 'ah' and 'ee', widen your mouth into a smile, but be aware that this will tend to make the tone slightly thinner. Practise both sounds along with Track 5.

CD 2: Track 5

Taking the 'ah' as a starting point, the vowel 'oo' is formed by bringing the lips forward (into a pout), which again can be done with the index finger still in position, so that the distance between the upper and lower front teeth remains constant. It is a good vowel on which to practise high notes, as it lessens the tendency to shout.

CD 2: Track 6

The other two Italian vowels are found between 'ah' and 'ee', and 'ee' and 'oo' respectively.

The easiest way to form 'eh' (as in 'May') is to start with 'ee', then flatten the tongue as if returning to 'ah'. 'Eh' will be reached when the tongue has left the front side teeth, but is still touching some back teeth. Try Track 7 which combines 'ee', 'eh' and 'ah'.

CD 2: Track 7

The easiest way to form 'aw' (as in 'more') is to start with 'ah', and then bring the lips forward as if forming an 'oo'. Try combining 'ah', 'aw' and 'oo' along with Track 8.

CD 2: Track 8

The thirteen vowel sounds that make up the English language can be seen as variations of these five basic Italian vowels.

Two basic four-note patterns

The following pattern of notes is known as an *arpeggio*.

CD 2: Track 9

If all four notes are sounded together, they produce a *major* chord, which you can hear on Track 10.

The major chord is one of the basic building blocks of music in the western classical tradition. The notes of the chord are often numbered 1, 3, and 5 (this refers to their positions within the *major scale*). As the top note has the same name as the bottom one, it is also numbered as 1.

Listen to Track 11 and then sing along to reinforce the numbering of the different 'degrees' of the chord:

CD 2: Track 11

piano x 4

1 3 5 1 5 3 1

You can use this pattern to make a really useful warm-up exercise. Sopranos and Tenors can sing along to Track 12 as it moves up through the keys. Altos and Basses should use Track 13.

CD 2: Track 12 - high voices

CD 2: Track 13 - low voices

Here's a different pattern, which mixes up the same chord degrees in a different order. Practise in the same way, transposing up through the keys.

CD 2: Track 14

piano

1 3 1 5 1 1 1 1 5 1 3 1 1 1

Exactly the same principles apply in a minor key – in fact, the only note that changes is number '3'. Listen to Track 15 and then sing along.

CD 2: Track 15

This numbering system is used instinctively by experienced singers to find notes. Master these exercises, so that the numbers become automatic, and you will find the note-finding cues in this edition invaluable.

Here is a rhythm exercise which will loosen up your voice for fast passages. It is based on a four-note phrase – the crotchets establish a basic pulse, the quavers divide that beat into two, the triplets divide it into three and the semi-quavers into four:

CD 2: Track 16

piano

La la la la *etc.*

3 3 3 3

Start off by singing 'la' to each note, and once you've mastered that, try using any one of the five Italian vowels.

If you wish, the exercise can be extended up through the keys – it's a great way of increasing breathing capacity and stamina, as well as developing your vocal agility.

Here's a variation of the same exercise that splits the pattern in half and repeats pairs of notes, forming a common 'trill' figure found throughout *Messiah* (and indeed, in many other compositions of the period).

CD 2: Track 17

Once again, this exercise can be practised in any key.

Intervals and note-finding

Those of us not blessed with perfect pitch have to rely on recognition of the different distances between notes (known as *intervals*), in order to know what to expect next. Although experience will, in most cases, allow you to make an intelligent guess, there are other techniques available to the amateur choral singer.

Let's imagine a musician's 'ruler' that is used to measure the distance between notes. 1 marks the note that we start on, so if we were to move to a note one step away (e.g. C to D) our ruler would read +2. (This may seem counter-intuitive to start with, but corresponds to the fact that the interval between C and D is known as a *2nd.*) Moving from C to E results in an interval of +3, moving from C to G is an interval of +5 and so on. Similarly, moving down from C to F would be measured as -5.

You've already used these interval numbers when singing major and minor arpeggios, but we can now extend the concept to identify all the other notes of the scale.

The following exercise will allow you to familiarise yourself with upward and downward leaping intervals. In turn, this should help you use the note-finding hints that you will find before each of your entries in the score.

CD 2: Track 18

This exercise can start on any note – the only limitation is your vocal range.

Experienced musicians often describe intervals in more detail (often using words like 'major', 'minor', 'perfect', 'augmented' and 'diminished'), but many singers enjoy a lifetime of choral singing without this degree of detail.

Practice and performance notes

The following notes on each chorus are intended as an aid to private study. The first three choruses are described in depth, with the intention that the techniques and strategies applied there can be applied to other choruses.

4. And The Glory Of The Lord

The opening theme (first sung by the Altos) is based round the major chord described in the 'warm-ups' section. Target each of the degrees of the chord (1, 3, & 5) to plot your way through this theme.

CD 2: Track 19

Handel expects the words 'glory' and 'of' to run into one another in an Italianate manner – as if the word were 'glaw-riof'. The 'riof' must be entirely smooth, and (unlike dotted rhythms elsewhere) not in any way articulated.

The second part of the theme consists of a repeated pattern – an upward leap of a 3rd followed by four descending notes of a scale.

CD 2: Track 20

The much-repeated figure demonstrated on Track 21 ('and all flesh') is just a variation of this second part of the theme – it's an upward leap of a 4th followed by four descending notes, back to the starting note.

CD 2: Track 21

7. And He Shall Purify

Take a look at the main theme of this chorus, as it appears in the Soprano part, and listen to Track 22:

CD 2: Track 22

Pay special attention to the grouping of the semi-quavers shown above by the square brackets – it doesn't coincide with the *musical* sequence of the passage, but it is a useful way of learning it (a trick employed by the famous pianist Busoni who called it *technical phrasing*).

When tackling difficult-looking passages like this, adopt a three-point plan:

1. Don't panic – passages like this often look more complex on the page than they really are.

2. Slow down! Practise slowly until you are totally secure.

3. Look at the phrase and deconstruct it – you will often find that a seemingly complicated passage can be broken down into little patterns which you might already recognise (or which are at least much easier to learn).

Let's apply this technique to the semi-quaver run in this passage (which occurs at a convenient pitch in bar 7 in the Basses, 11 in the Tenors and 48 in the Sopranos).

The first five-note pattern bracketed in the previous example can be broken into two easy patterns as follows:

1) the starting note, the note *above* and back :

CD 2: Track 23

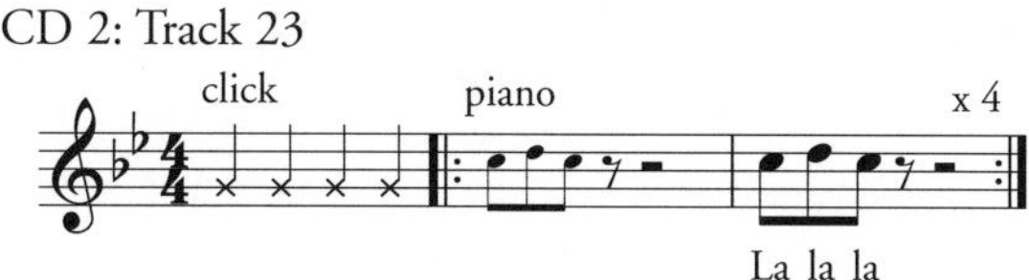

2) the starting note, the note *below* and back:

CD 2: Track 24

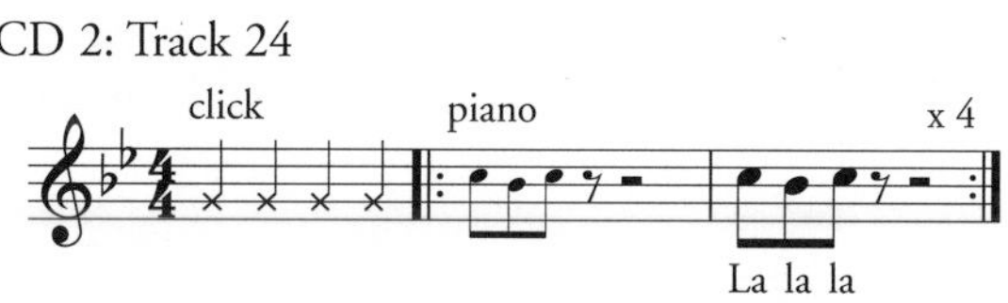

(Note values have been doubled for easier reading.)

When you can sing these two patterns along with Tracks 23 & 24 correctly, try running them one after another in time along with Track 25.

CD 2: Track 25

If you now remove the repeated C, you will find that you have learnt the first five-note pattern – often called a *turn*. Try singing it along with Track 26.

CD 2: Track 26

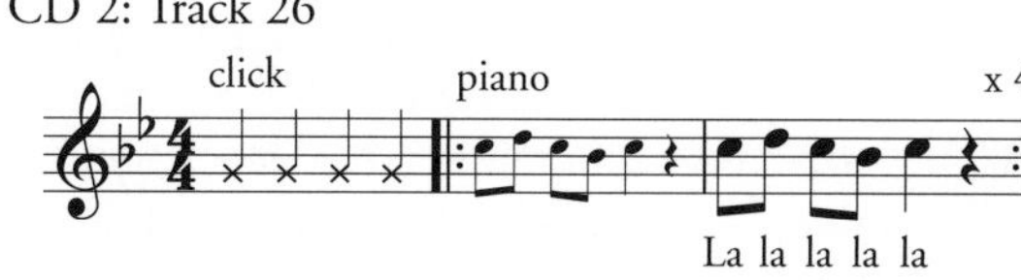

The next group of eight notes is reached by a drop of a 3rd, sounding like a cuckoo:

CD 2: Track 27

The second short pattern already learnt above (Track 24), also starts the second pattern of eight notes, starting on A instead of C:

CD 2: Track 28

This then leads into a slightly lower version of the five-note pattern already mastered (Track 26):

CD 2: Track 29

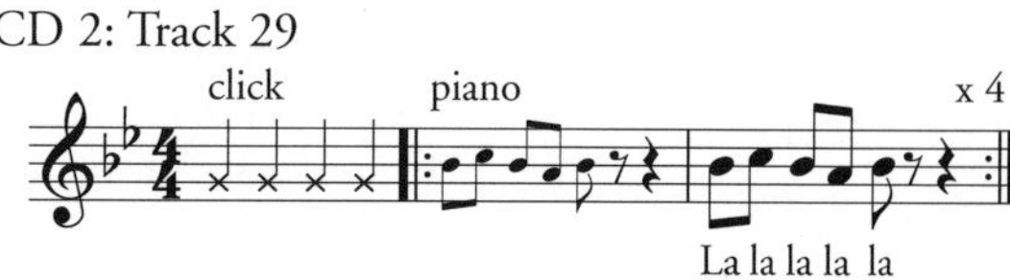

Add these two examples together to produce the full pattern:

CD 2: Track 30

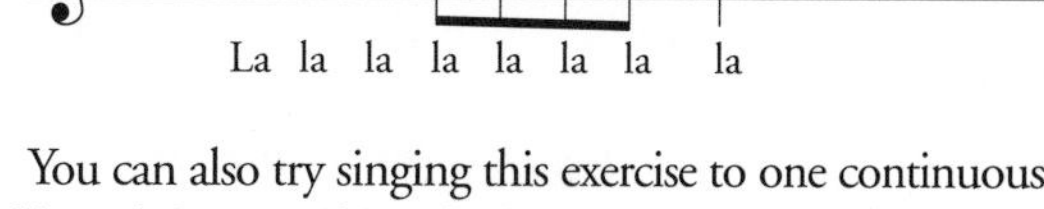

You can also try singing this exercise to one continuous 'ah', and then to 'fy' – the last syllable of 'purify'.

Having now learnt all the constituent elements of the semi-quaver passage, try the following exercise:

CD 2: Track 31

Finally, try singing along with the full version of the theme, this time as sung by the Basses.

CD 2: Track 32

basses - transcribed into treble clef
and he shall pu - ri - fy
the

9. O Thou That Tellest Good Tidings To Zion

In 6/8 each beat is a dotted crotchet, subdivided into three quavers, which can tend to feel unconnected. Try to feel the crotchet-quaver rhythm of each beat, at the same time being careful not to destroy the phrasing with ugly accentuation. Try saying the rhythm along with Track 33.

CD 2: Track 33

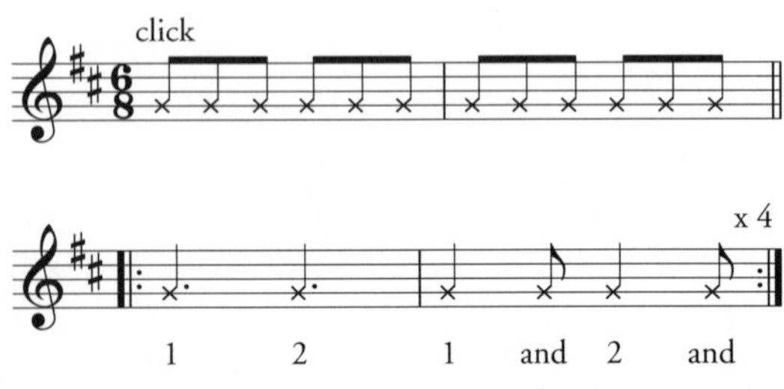
click
x 4
1 2 1 and 2 and

The other challenge in this chorus is the ornate figure which first occurs in the Alto part in bar 119. It is best learnt by building it up from a simplified version:

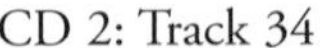
CD 2: Track 34

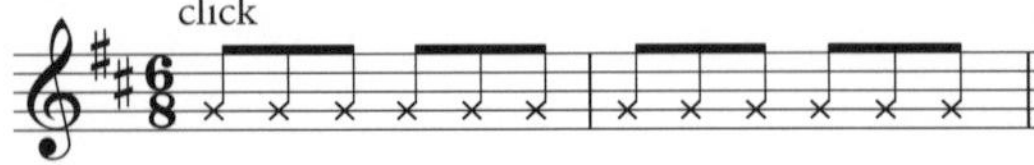
click

piano
Zi - on, a -

rise,
Zi - on, a -

rise,
Zi-on, a - rise

12. For Unto Us A Child Is Born

Once again, the repeated semi-quaver passages in this chorus tend to cause problems.

Start by mastering this simplified version:

CD 2: Track 35

click
La la la la etc.

Once you're happy with this, try singing along with Track 36 – a slowed-down version of the full theme.

CD 2: Track 36 – slowed down theme

basses - transcribed into treble clef
For un - to us a child is born

And finally, try the theme at full speed:

CD 2: Track 37 – theme at full speed

For the ultimate challenge to your vocal technique try singing every note to 'hah'!

Aim to keep the dotted note figures of 'and the government' rhythmic. The secret of singing dotted rhythms successfully is to think of the second note as leading into the next beat, rather than as coming after the dotted note. Try imagining the dot as a rest:

CD 2: Track 38

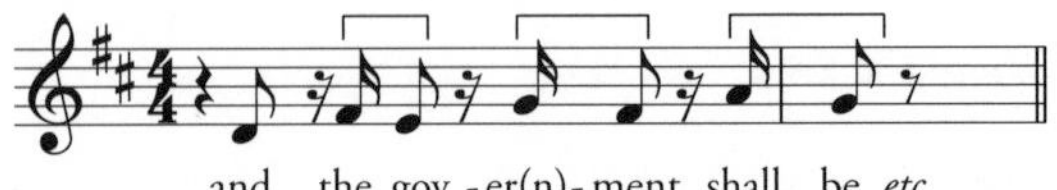
and the gov - er(n) - ment shall be etc.

17. Glory To God

The long opening notes of this chorus almost sing themselves, but the semi-quavers need to be given special effort as it is easy to lose them. However, accenting the semi-quavers must not distort the dotted rhythm.

The word 'Glory' is usually regarded as a two-syllable word, but in fact it has three! The first two happen so quickly that to most of us (apart from singers and actors who consider such matters in detail), they sound almost like one: 'Ge-law-ree'. Aim to get the second 'law' syllable on the beat with 'Ge' happening just before it. Practise this by singing 'Lawry to God'.

The phrase 'And peace on Earth' can also cause problems: firstly, the 'd' of 'and' can be completely inaudible; secondly the legato can be broken by sounding the 's' of peace, and the 'n' of 'on' too soon. The phrase therefore needs to be thought of as 'An deh pea soh nearth', with the 'deh' coming very quickly and as tight against the 'p' of 'peace' as possible:

CD 2: Track 39

The short motif of 'Goodwill towards men' needs to be tidy – with a precisely placed 'will'. Try singing an extra 'to' on the beat, as shown, or feel a very strong silent beat. There is sometimes a tendency to hold the tied note too long and then rush the semi-quavers to catch up, or conversely jump too soon off the tied note, and slow the semi-quavers so that they almost degenerate into triplet quavers.

CD 2: Track 40

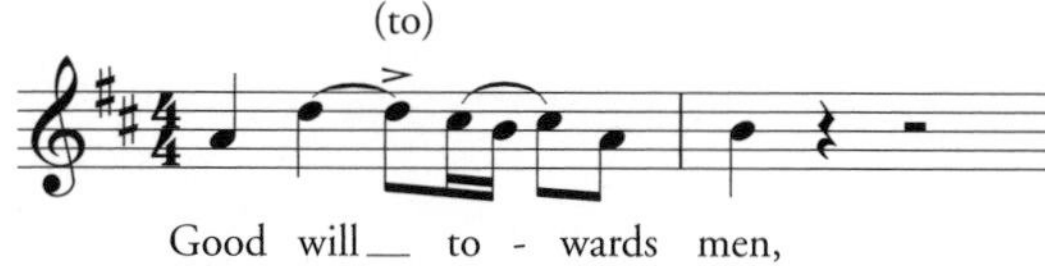

21. His Yoke Is Easy, And His Burthen Is Light

At first, the main theme from this chorus looks challenging, but if you follow through Tracks 41-51 you should find that its individual parts are no more complicated than anything else in the work.

The first phrase is based around the major chord pattern. First try this simplified version:

CD 2: Track 41

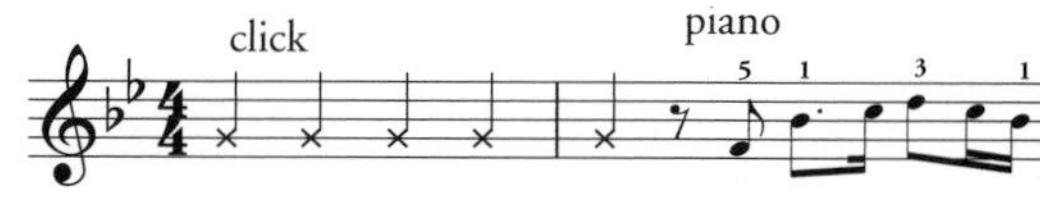

Then fill in the gaps:

CD 2: Track 42

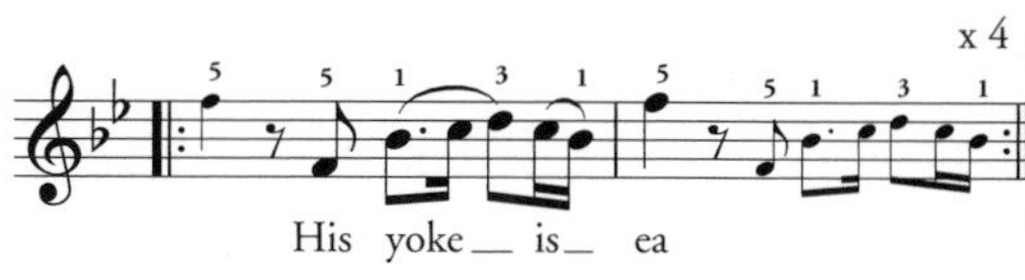

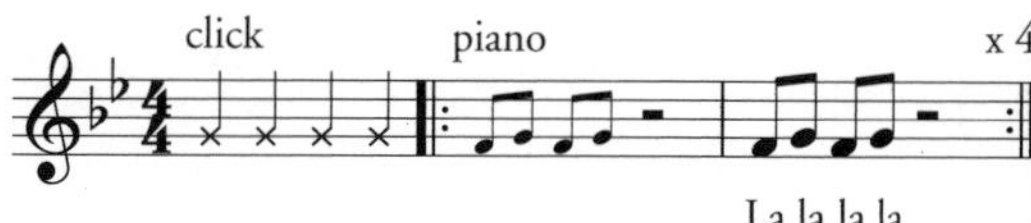

The second part of the first half of the phrase, which looks complicated, can be built up gradually, by putting together Tracks 43-50. Start with this simple alternating figure:

CD 2: Track 43

Next, add a downward 'cuckoo' jump:

CD 2: Track 44

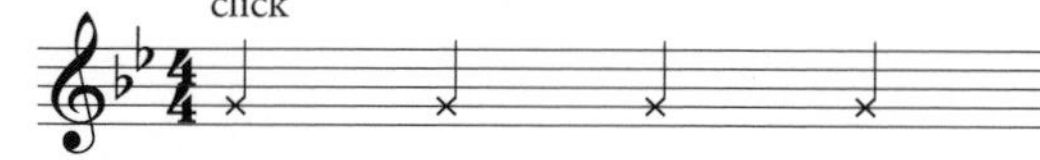

And now combine Tracks 43 and 44 to form this mini-phrase:

CD 2: Track 45

Now let's put Tracks 42 and 45 together to form the first half of the theme:

CD 2: Track 46

Now let's tackle the second half of the phrase. Once again, start simply:

CD 2: Track 47

Once you've mastered this *inverted turn*, add a dotted rhythm to the first two quavers:

CD 2: Track 48

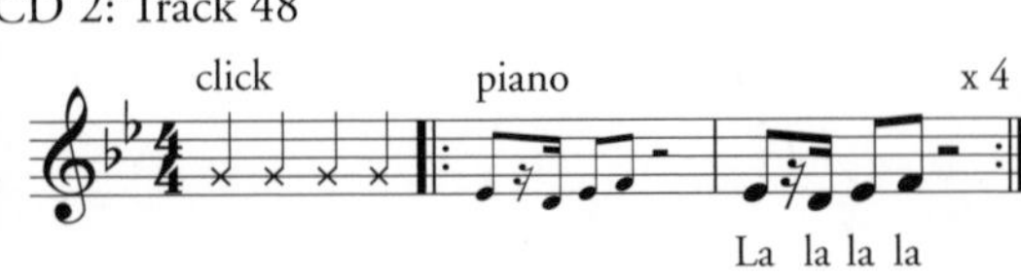

The next component should be familiar to you by now – it's a stepwise figure like others that we have encountered in previous choruses:

CD 2: Track 49

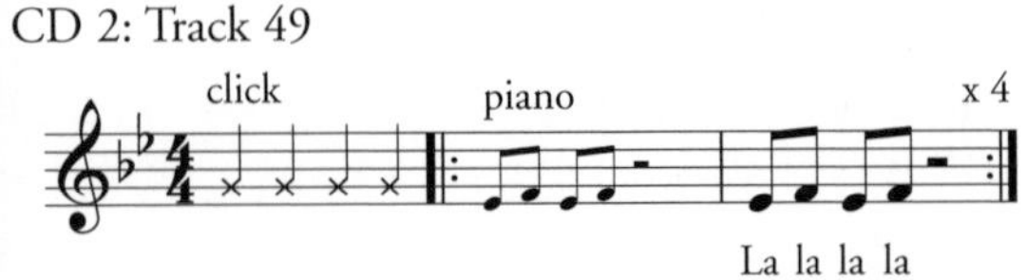

Next, we have a descending three-note figure, which may remind you of a certain well-known nursery rhyme!

CD 2: Track 50

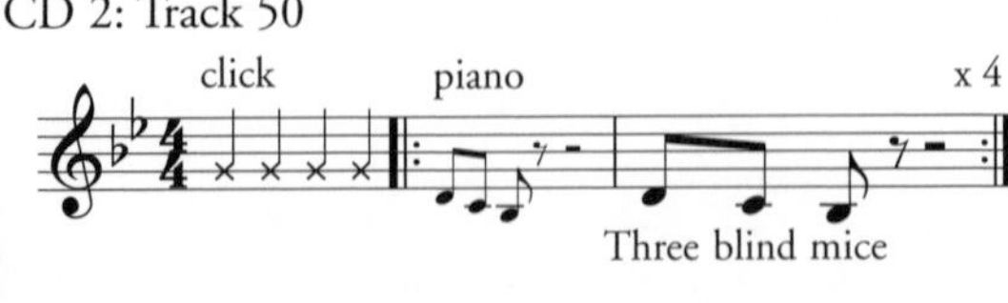

Once you've mastered Tracks 48-50, these three mini-phrases can be put together to form the second half of the main phrase:

CD 2: Track 51

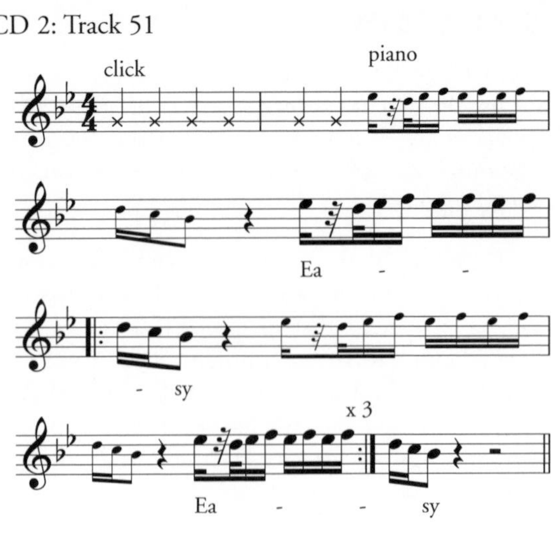

And finally, put the two halves of the phrase together to create this complete theme:

CD 2: Track 52

At the very end of the chorus you might need to gently drop out, take an extra breath, and ease your way in again. Listen to your immediate neighbours and try to stagger the process to avoid an unwanted gap!

Always phrase 'burthen' with a graceful *diminuendo* (it's surprising how quiet the second syllable needs to be). Remember that in practice *diminuendo* means 'loud getting quieter', so 'bur' needs to be loud enough to start with – you can't get quieter if you're already as quiet as possible!

22. Behold The Lamb Of God

This looks deceptively easy on the page. The rhythm needs to be tight – think of the short notes as both leading to, and being as close as possible to, the following long note.

The large octave leaps can have the effect of opening up the rhythm. Likewise, the tongue-twisting double 't' required for 'that taketh' requires detailed practice: try building it up by saying 'take' to a steady beat, then add 'that' as close as possible, aiming to keep the tight rhythm but avoiding 'tha taketh' (missing off the 't' on that). The percussive effect of this double 't' is part of the charm of this chorus.

Say the words through in time and then sing along to Track 53.

CD 2: Track 53

24. Surely He Hath Borne Our Griefs

Handel was originally German, (spelling his name Händel) and is sometimes accused of not fully understanding the niceties of accentuation of the English language. However, in this movement he demonstrates one of the cleverest word setting tricks in the whole of the choral and song repertoire, opening out the two syllable word 'surely' into three syllables (shoor-reh-lee). To the singer this might at first seem slightly odd, but to the listener it sounds amazingly natural, avoiding the tendency towards singing on the 'r' of 'surely', which is guaranteed to hinder good vocal tone.

Practise along with Track 54, and then insert the 'reh', as in Track 55, making sure that the 'reh-lee' is tight. You may be surprised at how much lighter the 'lee' needs to be than the 'shoor' to achieve graceful phrasing.

CD 2: Track 54

CD 2: Track 55

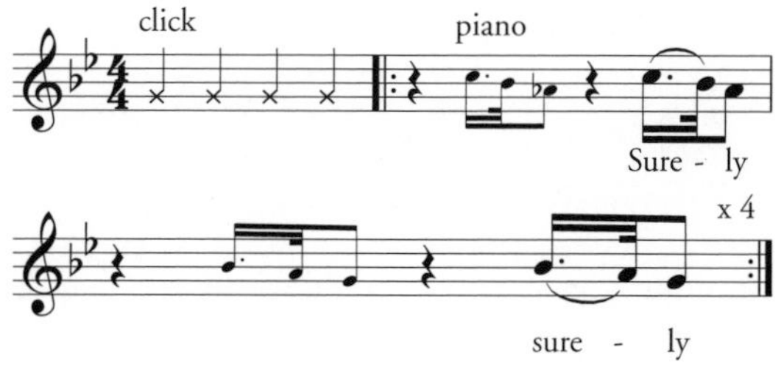

The setting of the words 'He was bruised fo transgressions, He was bruised for our iniquities – arguably the most theologically significant in the whole work – uses wonderfully rich harmonies with incredible voice progressions, especially in the Alto and Tenor parts. Listen carefully to make sure you are fitting in with the required blend of sound.

25. And With His Stripes We Are Healed

This fugue has two versions of the main theme (known as the *subject*) – the first two notes leap down in the Soprano and Tenor opening versions but move by step in the opening Alto and Bass versions. Watch the tuning of the leap between 'his' and 'stripes'.

CD 2: Track 56

CD 2: Track 57

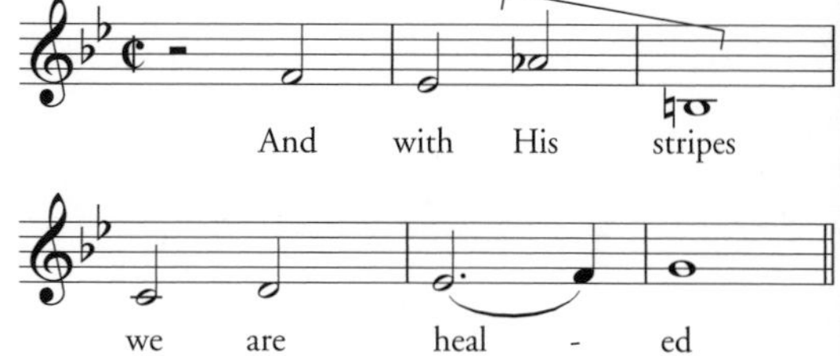

The *counter-subject* (so-called because it always appears with the *subject* and is in contrast with it), consists of an upward leap (+4) followed by a descending scale.

CD 2: Track 58

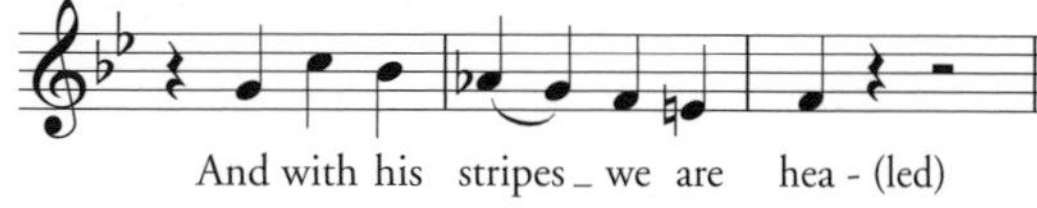

While a fugue may seem complicated, once you have mastered the three themes above, you have really dealt with most of the difficulties in one go. All you have to do now is avoid the temptation to move too early or too late as other parts move at different times around you.

Word underlay varies between editions, so pencil in any variants your conductor might require.

26. All We Like Sheep Have Gone Astray

Pay careful attention to Handel's charming word-painting on 'turned'. This rather intimidating looking string of semi-quavers consists of six turn-like figures. Each figure contains a short scale and a leap: the first pattern comes three times; the second group of four semi-quavers is the same a step down, while the fourth and last group of four semi-quavers are the same.

Start by mastering the first group to 'la':

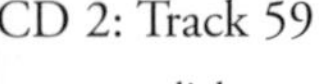
CD 2: Track 59

Then try the last group:

CD 2: Track 60

Now try a slowed-down version of the complete theme to 'la', then to 'ah', and finally with the correct words:

CD 2: Track 61

And finally try the phrase at the correct speed:

CD 2: Track 62 - full speed version

28. He Trusted In God That He Would Deliver Him

It is thought that writing in horizontal lines – known as *counterpoint* – may have been a way of creating harmony without breaking strict churchmen's rules which at one time decreed that words could only be set to one melody, which should, as far as possible, reflect natural spoken inflections. In a good performance, the listener should be able to hear all the entries of the subject, as it passes from voice to voice. The rests, and in this number the percussive 't's in the words 'trusted' and 'delight' therefore need to be made clear, so that they sound almost like cymbals. Likewise, the 'H ' of 'He' should be given plenty of 'Heh'.

Whenever themes are nearly the same, it is important to be very clear as to where the differences occur. The two versions of the subject (altered to fit the harmony) are distinguished by the interval between the first two notes. The first version has a drop of a fifth:

CD 2: Track 63

Whereas the second version has a drop of a fourth:

CD 2: Track 64

Notice too that the second theme ('Let Him deliver Him') has two different versions. The first version features a fourth followed by a descending scale:

CD 2: Track 65

The second version, however, repeats the top note:

CD 2: Track 66

In both cases aim for the 'li' of 'deliver', and then *diminuendo*.

33. Lift Up Your Heads, O Ye Gates

The dotted rhythms here present the same challenges as found in 'Behold The Lamb Of God'.

The rhythm needs to be taut, with no rushing anywhere within it. Practise tapping it on a table top, then say the words, and finally sing along:

CD 2: Track 67

Look out also for the end of the word 'hosts', which needs to be together – place the 'sts' on the following rest.

35. Let All The Angels Of God Worship Him

Handel's setting of the word 'worship' – especially in the very opening – captures the natural *crescendo* from the 'w' into the first vowel, as in the word 'Whoosh'.

The main theme is varied after its first appearance, and contains the main difficulty: the precise rhythm. Practise in the same way as you would any other tricky rhythm – first, tap out the rhythm, then say it, and finally, sing it:

CD 2: Track 68

37. The Lord Gave The Word

The precise rhythm of the phrase 'The Lord gave the Word' can be achieved by feeling the fourth beat and then putting 'the' as close as possible to 'Word'. Make sure that the 'd' of 'Lord' doesn't come too early and cut off the sound – think of 'Law-deh gave', placing the 'deh' tightly against 'gave'.

CD 2: Track 69

A little rolled 'r' within the words 'great' and 'preachers' makes for both good singing tone as well as natural phrasing.

The strings of semi-quavers mostly consist of short alternating figures, such as those already seen in 'His Yoke Is Easy...' – however, a new challenge is the repeated note within the ascending scale in the figure below:

CD 2: Track 70

The repeated semi-quavers must not be tied together (as if they were a quaver), but rather should be clearly enunciated.

39. Their Sound Is Gone Out Into All Lands

In this chorus, you should aim to create smooth rhythmical quaver scales with consistent tone, and graceful phrasing.

The Tenors sing this elegant passage at letter A, complete with E naturals:

CD 2: Track 71

But Sopranos need to watch out, because when their entry comes two bars later, there are some unexpected E flats:

CD 2: Track 72

Altos are given the same test eight and nine bars after B, with an unexpected A flat either side of the crotchet top B flat. Basses sing the more obvious version in parallel with the sopranos a couple of bars later.

41. Let Us Break Their Bonds Asunder

As an illustration of the word 'break', the opening quaver figure should be sung *staccato* whenever it comes.

The word 'way' can be made really lively by breaking the quavers:

CD 2: Track 73

Notice that the string of eight semi-quavers consists of two turns, repeated in the next bar.

44. Hallelujah!

George II was so impressed with the magnificence of this chorus that he stood up, and the audience followed suit, thereby starting a tradition which knowledgeable audiences have continued to this day.

The long notes almost sing themselves, so extra emphasis needs to be given to the quavers and semi-quavers – especially those which are off the beat. The rhythm throughout needs to be precise, underpinned with a really strong beat. Tap a strict beat, say the words in time, and then sing along with Track 74.

CD 2: Track 74

Sometimes 'Hallelujah' is mispronounced with an extra 'l' – the correct pronunciation is 'Ha-lay-loo-yah' (not 'lool-yah'). Make sure that you put plenty of effort into the first 'H', especially when it is off the beat.

It is important to count bars such as the pair before B, where it is all too easy to miss out a 'Hallelujah'. Equally it is all too easy to give your colleagues an unscheduled and unwanted solo in the last six bars with an extra one! Accurate counting and big breaths are also required for the semi-breve 'Lords' and 'Kings'.

Watch out for unmarked but often performed tempo changes. Letter C will often be broadened, until D, where it speeds up to the original tempo. The final 'Hallelujah' is usually performed *Adagio*.

46. Since By Man Came Death

Firstly, note that the two fast sections start differently. The first starts after you have counted 'one-two' – i.e. on the half beat. Try practising along with Track 75 – the first four times, say the words in the correct rhythm; the second four times sing along with the choir:

CD 2: Track 75

The second section, however, starts directly on the second beat:

CD 2: Track 76

The opening quaver(s) need to be strong and confident to achieve a contrast between these and the preceding slow sustained *Grave* bars.

The two *Grave* sections need to be sung smoothly, quietly and of course, in tune, which can be a problem, as the chorus will be beginning to tire by this stage of the performance (some conductors ask the quartet of soloists to sing these sections for this reason).

All of this is easier said than done, and this is one of those passages which really tests the mettle of the singers. The starting point is breath control, so that there is always plenty of breath in reserve, even after the Alto and Tenor crotchets settle on the last chord.

When we sing or talk, we hear our own voices differently to other people's because, as well as receiving sound through the vibration of air, we also hear ourselves via our skull bones – which can sometimes impair judgement of tuning. Try cutting out this 'skull hearing' by putting your index finger in one ear and very gently pulling your finger forward.

51. But Thanks Be To God

The number of 'thanks' are potentially tongue twisting – the best form of preparatory practice is to tap a strict beat and say the words through in time to it. The figure below needs to be rhythmical and can be learnt by singing each note to 'la':

CD 2: Track 77

53a. Worthy Is The Lamb That Was Slain

Watch out for the various speed changes here.

If you master the opening Tenor and Bass figure below, you will have covered the basis of all the semi-quaver passages in this section. The key to controlling this section is feeling strong second and third beats.

CD 2: Track 78

The 'ry' of 'Glory' runs straight into 'and', as if the word were 'Glaw-riand', with 'riand' sung perfectly smoothly.

53b. Amen

Look out for varying degrees of *rallentando* from letter L to the end, depending on your conductor. Watch your conductor especially carefully from bars 9 and 10 after L to check when to start, and how fast to sing the quaver runs. Be vigilant from here to the end, as it is at this point in a long performance (perhaps also following a demanding rehearsal), just when everyone is in sight of the final bars, that concentration levels can lapse. The performance is not over until the applause starts.

And finally...

The editor hopes that these guidelines have not only helped you to sing Handel's *Messiah* with confidence, but have also demonstrated a useful approach to preparing any work. You should by now have realised that the secret to efficient learning is patiently to master small pieces stage by stage before assembling the larger building blocks of the music.

Set small realistic targets for each practice session. Schedule a finish time for each rehearsal, so that at the end of it you can be clear about what you have achieved – you should therefore be encouraged to repeat the experience.

A practice session of only five minutes in which you master a couple of awkward bars is a worthwhile achievement. In fact, six ten-minute sessions throughout the week prior to the concert will probably be far more productive than an hour-long panic session the night before – the most noticeable achievement will probably be your tired voice.

The only hindrance to the enjoyment of singing is your conscience telling you that you haven't done enough preparation. So, if you have methodically worked your way through these notes, the last piece of advice is to get out there and enjoy it!

1 Overture

2 Recitative – Comfort Ye My People (Tenor)

Comfort ye My people
Saith your God.
Speak ye comfortably to Jerusalem
And cry unto her
That her warfare is accomplished
That her iniquity is pardoned.

The voice of him that crieth in the wilderness
'Prepare ye the way of the Lord
Make straight in the desert
A highway for our God.'

3 Air – Every Valley Shall Be Exalted (Tenor)

Every valley shall be exalted,
And every mountain and hill made low
The crooked straight and the rough places plain.

4 Chorus – And The Glory Of The Lord

CD1 Track 1 CD2 Tracks 19-21

EP 10 P 10 WS 11

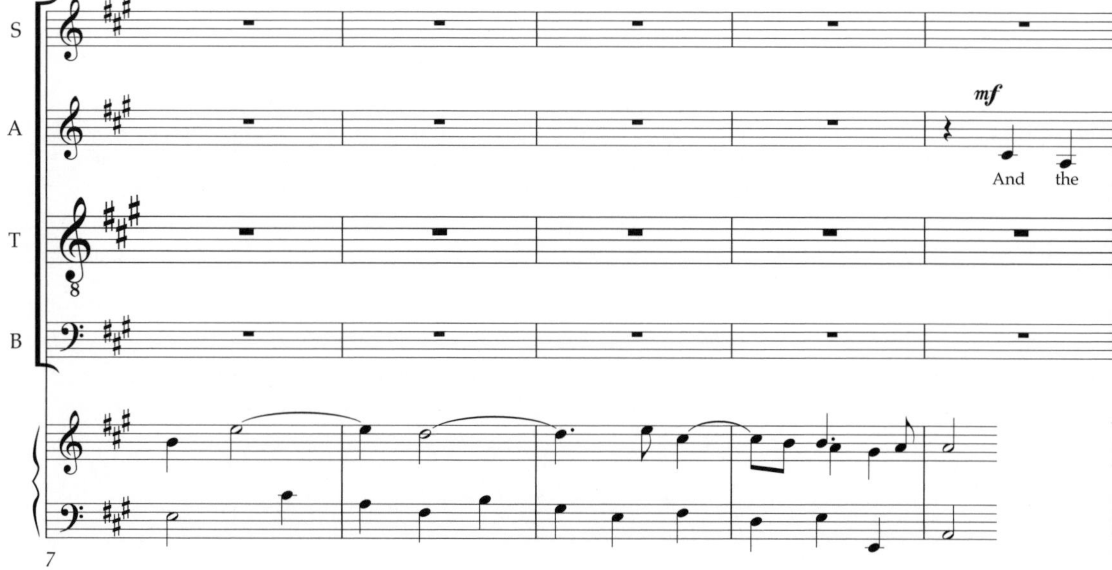

f
And the glo - ry, the glo - ry of the
f
glo - ry, the glo - ry of the Lord, the glo - ry of the
-4
f
And the glo - ry, the glo - ry of the
f
And the glo - ry, the glo - ry of the
12
P
WS
11
12
mf
Lord shall be re -
Lord
mf
Lord shall be re - veal - - - ed,
mf
Lord shall be re - veal - - -
17
EP
11
- veal - - - - ed, and the glo - ry, the
mf
shall be re -
=
and the glo - ry, the glo - ry of the Lord
- ed, shall be re - veal - ed,
22

glo - ry of the Lord shall
- veal - ed, be re - veal - - - - - - - - - - - -
=
shall be re - veal - - - ed,
27
A
be re - veal'd, and the glo - ry, the glo - ry of the Lord shall be
- - - ed, and the glo - ry, the glo - ry of the Lord shall be
-3
and the glo - ry, the glo - ry of the Lord shall be
and the glo - ry, the glo - ry of the Lord shall be
32
P
WS
12
13
re - veal - ed,
re - veal - - ed,
re - veal - ed,
re - veal - - ed,
37

mf
and all flesh shall see it to - ge - ther,
-5
42
12
B
mf
and all flesh shall see it to - ge - ther,
f
for
f
for
47
13
14
f
and all flesh shall see it to - ge - - -
f
and all flesh shall see it to - - - ge -
the mouth of the Lord hath spo - ken
the mouth of the Lord hath spo - ken
52

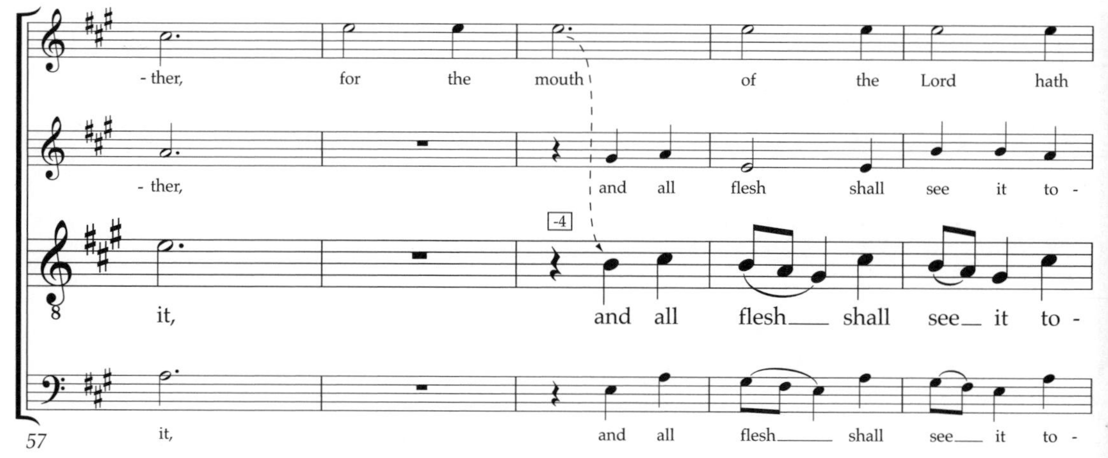
-4
- ther, for the mouth of the Lord hath
- ther, and all flesh shall see it to -
it, and all flesh shall see it to -
it, and all flesh shall see it to -
57

spo - ken it,
mf
- ge - - - ther, and all flesh, and all flesh shall
-2
mf
- ge - - - ther, and all flesh shall see it to -
- ge - - - ther,
62

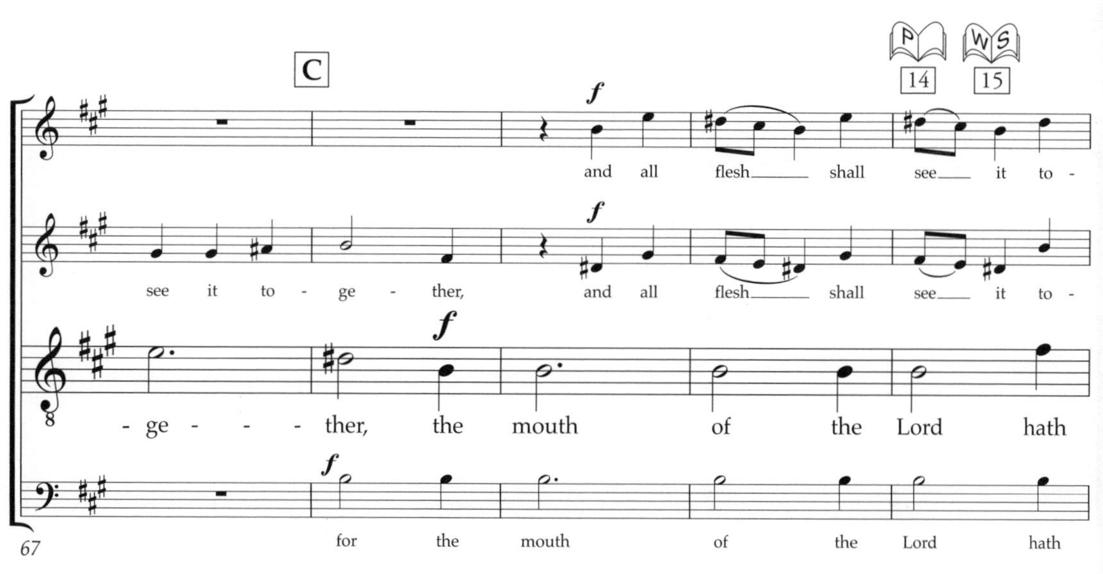
C
P
14
WS
15
f
and all flesh shall see it to -
f
see it to - ge - ther, and all flesh shall see it to -
f
- ge - - - ther, the mouth of the Lord hath
f
for the mouth of the Lord hath
67

13
- ge - - - - ther, and the
- ge - - - - ther, and the
spo - ken it, and the
spo - ken it, and the
72
glo - ry, the glo - ry of the Lord, and all flesh shall
glo - ry, the glo - ry of the Lord, and all flesh shall see
glo - ry, the glo-ry of the Lord, and all flesh shall see it, shall
glo - ry, the glo - ry of the Lord, and all flesh shall
77
D
see it to - ge - ther, the mouth of the Lord hath
it to - ge - ther, and the glo - ry, the glo - ry of the
see it to - ge - ther,
see it to - ge - ther,
82

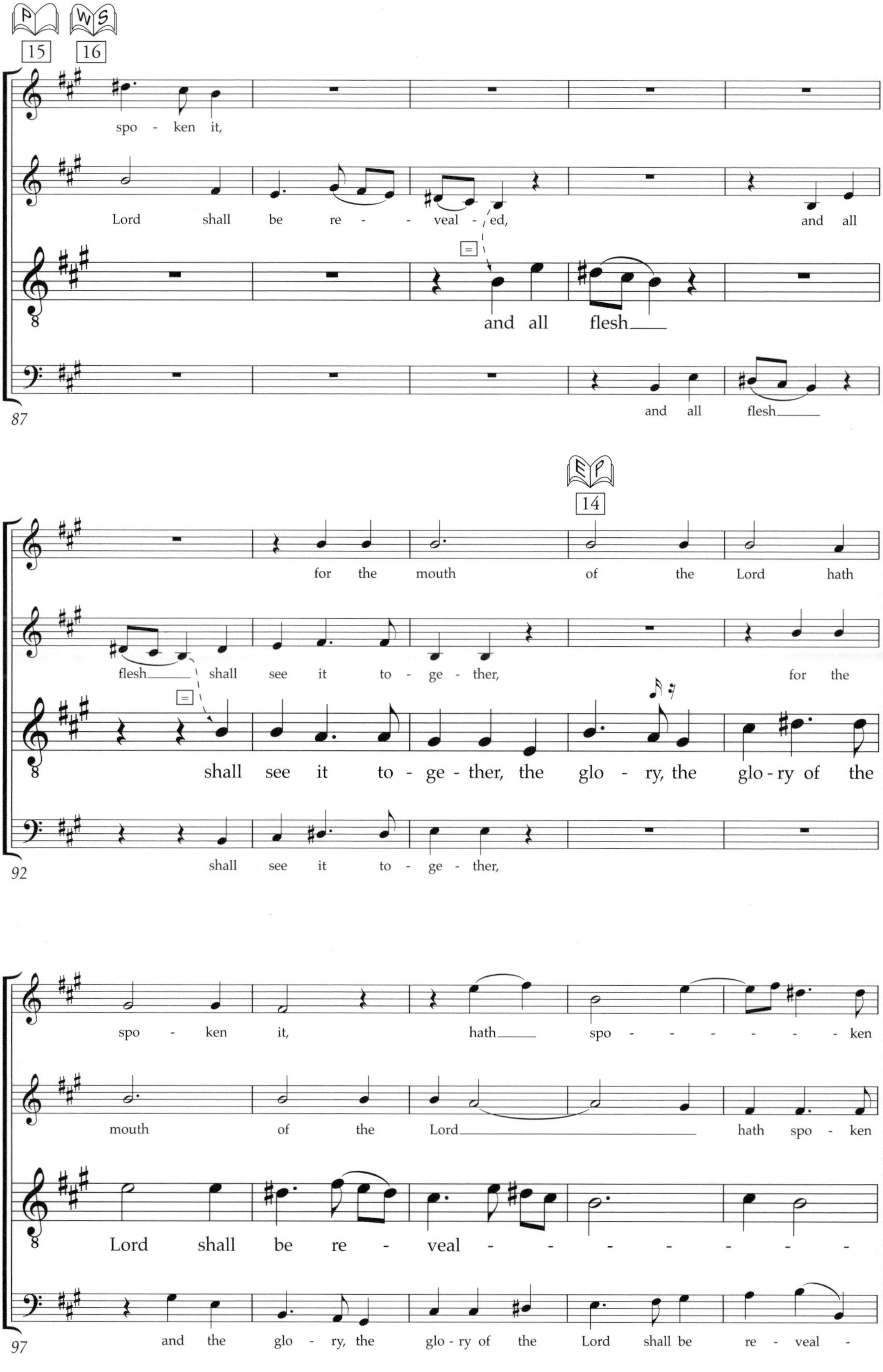

15 16

spo - ken it,

Lord shall be re - - veal - ed, and all

and all flesh

and all flesh

87

14

for the mouth of the Lord hath

flesh shall see it to - ge - ther, for the

shall see it to - ge - ther, the glo - ry, the glo - ry of the

shall see it to - ge - ther,

92

E
16
17
ff
it, and the
it, and all flesh shall see it to -
- ed, and all flesh shall see it to-
- ed, and all flesh shall see it to -
102

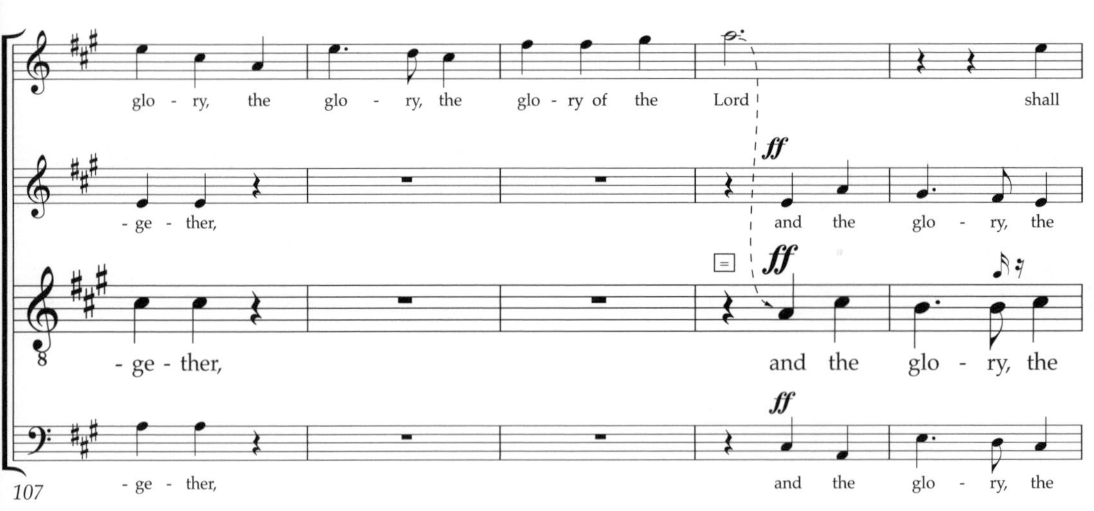
glo - ry, the glo - ry, the glo - ry of the Lord shall
ff
- ge - ther, and the glo - ry, the
ff
- ge - ther, and the glo - ry, the
ff
- ge - ther, and the glo - ry, the
107

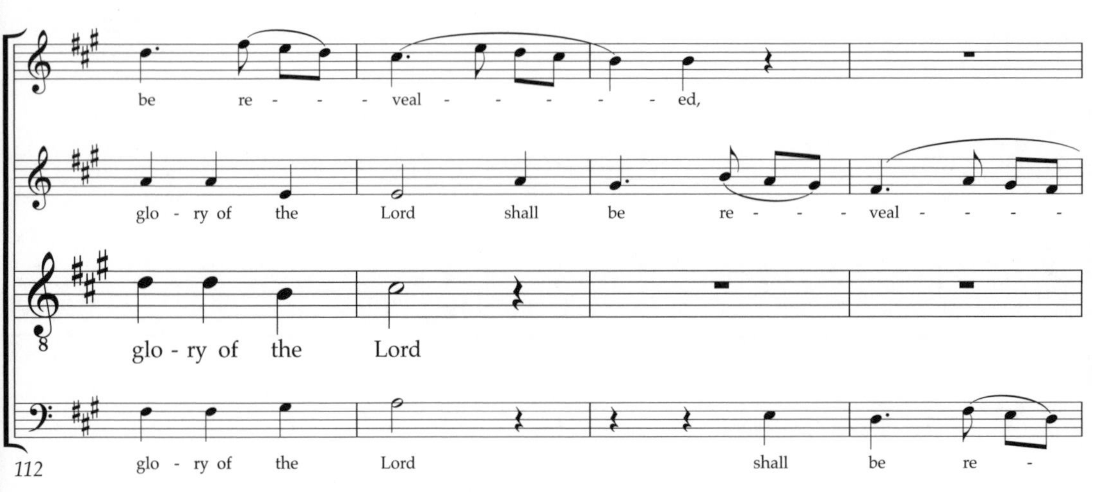
be re - - - veal - - - - - - ed,
glo - ry of the Lord shall be re - - - veal - - - -
glo - ry of the Lord
glo - ry of the Lord shall be re -
112

15
and all flesh shall
- ed, re - veal - ed, and all flesh shall
shall be re - veal - ed, and all flesh shall
116
- veal - - - - ed, re - veal - - - ed, for the mouth
17
18
F
1
see it to - ge - ther, to - ge - - - - ther, for the mouth
see it to - ge - ther, to - ge - - - - ther; for the
-4
5
see it to - ge - ther, to - ge - - - ther; for the
121
of the Lord hath spo - ken it, for the
of the Lord hath spo - ken it, for the
mouth of the Lord hath spo - ken it, for the
mouth of the Lord hath spo - ken it,
126
mouth of the Lord hath spo - ken it,

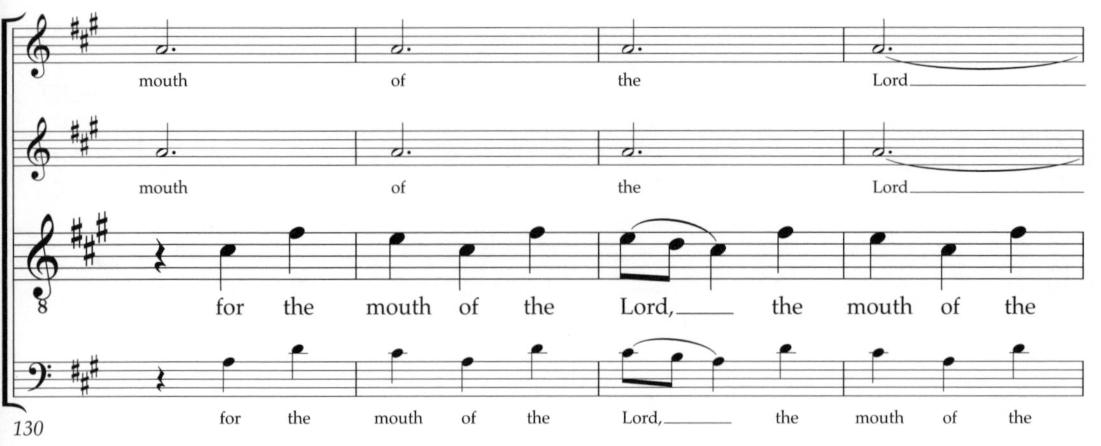

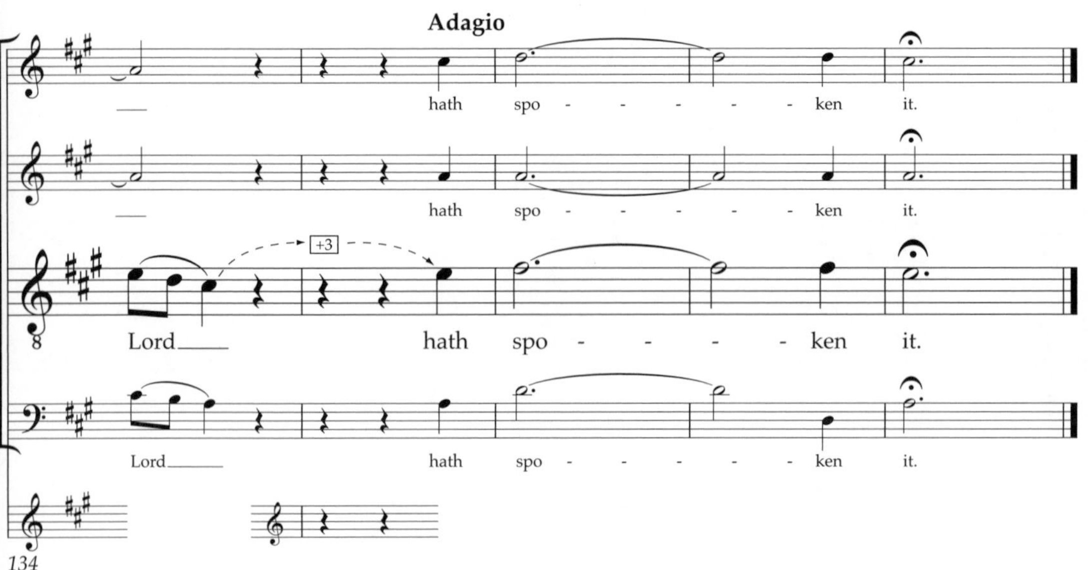

5 Recitative – Thus Saith The Lord (Bass)

Thus saith the Lord, the Lord of Hosts;
Yet once, a little while
And I will shake the heavens
And the earth, the sea, and the dry land.
And I will shake all nations
I'll shake the heavens
The earth, the sea, the dry land
All nations, I'll shake
And the desire of all nations shall come.

The Lord, whom ye seek, shall suddenly come to His temple
Even the messenger of the covenant, whom ye delight in
Behold, He shall come, saith the Lord of Hosts.

6 Air – But Who May Abide The Day Of His Coming? (Alto)

But who may abide the day of His coming?
And who shall stand when He appeareth?
For He is like a refiner's fire
Who shall stand when He appeareth?

7 Chorus – And He Shall Purify

Allegro ♩ = 92

mf

S
And He shall pu - ri - fy, and He shall pu - ri - fy

A

T

B

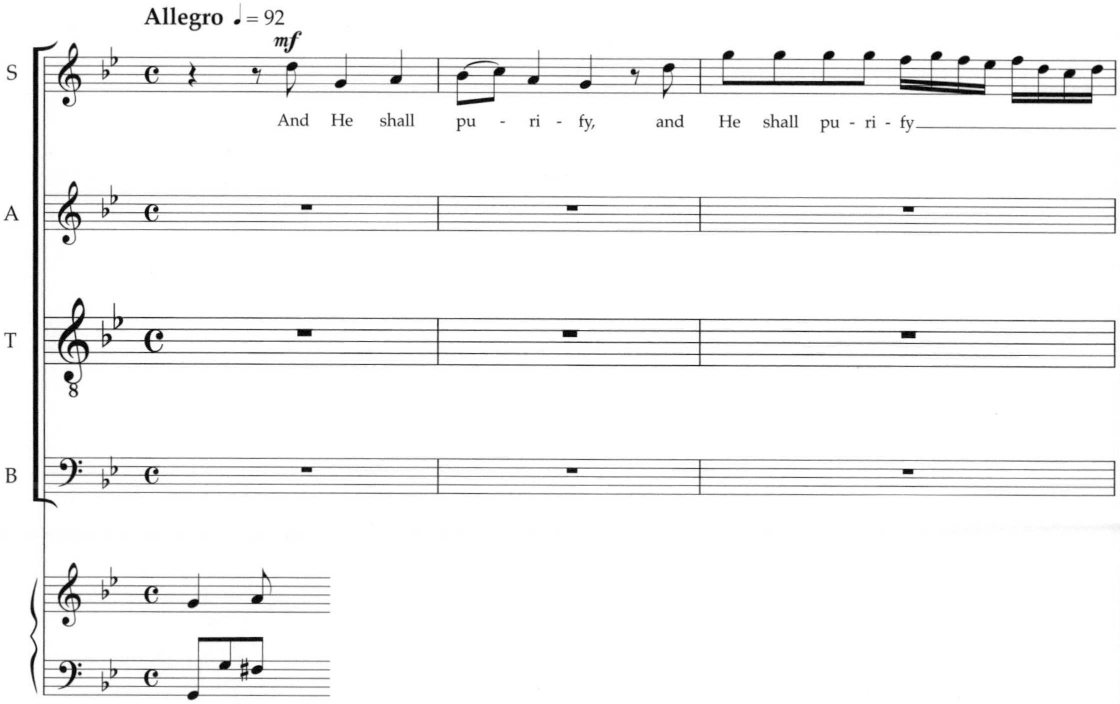

25
mf
And He shall
He shall pu - ri - fy
the sons of
7
28
36
A
pu - ri - fy,
and
-4
mf
And He shall pu-ri-fy
the sons
Le - vi,
10
f
and He shall pu-ri-
He shall pu-ri-fy
of Le - - - vi,
f
and
13

- fy the sons of Le - - - - -
the sons of Le - - - - vi,
+2
f
and He shall pu-ri-fy
He shall pu - ri - fy, and He shall pu - ri - fy the sons of Le - - - - -
16
29
37
26
B
- vi, the sons of Le - vi, that they may of - fer
the sons of Le - vi, that they may of - fer
the sons of Le - vi, that they may of - fer
- vi, the sons, the sons of Le - vi, that they may of - fer
19
un - to the Lord an of - fer - ing in right - eous - ness, in right - eous -
un - to the Lord an of - fer - ing in right - eous - ness, in right - eous-
un - to the Lord an of - fer - ing in right - eous - ness, in right - eous-
un - to the Lord an of - fer - ing in right - eous - ness, in right - eous-
22

mf
- ness, and He shall pu - ri - fy,
f
- ness, and He shall pu - ri - fy,
-3
f
- ness, and He shall pu - ri - fy,
f
mf
- ness, and He shall pu - ri - fy, shall pu - ri -
25
P
WS
EP
30
38
27
mf
and He shall pu - ri -
f
and He shall pu - ri - fy,
f
=
and He shall pu - ri - fy,
f
- fy the sons of Le - vi,
28
C
f
- fy, shall pu - ri - fy,
f
and He shall pu - ri - fy,
=
f
and He shall pu - ri - fy,
f
and He shall pu - ri - fy,
31

and He shall pu - ri - fy,
and He shall pu - ri -
and He shall pu - ri - fy,
and He shall pu - ri - fy,
and
and He shall pu - ri - fy,
and He shall pu - ri - fy the sons of
34
31
39
- fy the sons, the sons of Le - vi,
and He shall
and He shall pu - ri - fy,
He shall pu - ri - fy the sons of Le - vi,
and He shall
Le - vi, the sons of Le - vi,
and He shall
37
D
28
pu - ri - fy,
and He shall pu - ri - fy
the sons
-5
pu - ri - fy,
and He shall pu - ri - fy
pu - ri - fy,
and He shall pu - ri - fy, shall pu - ri -
40

and He shall pu - ri - fy,
of Le - vi,
the sons of Le - vi,
- fy the sons of Le - vi, the sons
43
32
40
and He shall pu - ri - fy
shall pu - ri - fy, shall pu - ri - fy,
shall pu-ri-fy the sons
of Le - - - vi, and
46
29
the sons of Le - vi,
shall pu - ri - fy the sons of Le - vi,
of Le - - - - - - - vi, the sons of Le - vi,
He shall pu - ri - fy the sons, the sons of Le - vi,
49

8 Recitative – Behold, A Virgin Shall Conceive (Alto)

Behold, a virgin shall conceive, and bear a son
And shall call His name Emmanuel:
'God with us'.

9 Air and Chorus – O Thou That Tellest Good Tidings To Zion (Alto)

O thou that tellest good tidings to Zion
Get thee up into the high mountain.

O thou that tellest good tidings to Jerusalem
Lift up thy voice with strength.

Lift it up, be not afraid
Say unto the cities of Judah
Behold your God!

O thou that tellest good tidings to Zion
Arise, shine, for thy light is come
And the glory of the Lord is risen upon thee.

9 Air and Chorus – O Thou That Tellest Good Tidings To Zion

I
ti - dings to Zi - on, good ti - dings to Zi - on, a - rise, a -
Zi - - - on, a - rise, a -
thou that tell - est good ti - dings to Zi - on, a - rise, a -
-3
a - rise, a -
113
P
WS
39
47
- rise, say un - to the cit - ies of Ju - dah, Be - hold your God! Be -
- rise, say un - to the cit - ies of Ju - dah, Be - hold your God! Be -
- rise, say un - to the cit - ies of Ju - dah, Be - hold your God! Be -
+3
-4
- rise, say un - to the cit - ies of Ju - dah, Be - hold your God! Be -
116
- hold, the glo - ry of the Lord is
- hold, the glo - ry of the Lord is
- hold, the glo - ry of the Lord is
+3
- hold, the glo - ry of the Lord is
120

EP
36
K
P
40
WS
48
ris - en up - on thee, O thou that tell - est good ti - dings to Zi - on, say
ris - en up - on thee, O thou that tell - est good ti - dings to Zi - on, say
ris-en up - on thee, O thou that tell-est good ti-dings to Zi-on, say
ris - en up - on thee, O thou that tell - est good ti - dings to Zi - on, say
123
un - to the cit - ies of Ju - dah, be - hold, be -
un - to the cit - ies of Ju - dah, be - hold, be -
un - to the cit - ies of Ju - dah, be - hold, -3 be -
un - to the cit - ies of Ju - dah, be - hold, be -
127
- hold, the glo - ry of the Lord, of the Lord,
- hold, the glo - ry of the Lord, of the Lord, the
- hold, -4 the glo - ry of the Lord, of the Lord,
- hold, the glo - ry of the Lord, of the Lord,
130

10 Recitative – For Behold, Darkness Shall Cover The Earth (Bass)

For behold, darkness shall cover the earth
And gross darkness the people
But the Lord shall arise upon thee
And His glory shall be seen upon thee
And the Gentiles shall come to thy light
And kings to the brightness of thy rising.

11 Air – The People That Walked In Darkness (Bass)

The people that walked in darkness
Have seen a great light
And they that dwell
In the land of the shadow of death
Upon them hath the light shined.

12 Chorus – For Unto Us A Child Is Born

2 47 55

Andante allegro ♩ = 94

4

A

p

For un - to us a Child is born, un - to us a Son is

7

43
5
giv-en, un-to us a Son is giv-en, for un-to
-5
p
1
For un-to us a Child is born,
10
48
56
3
us a Child is born:
-3
1
=
+4
un-to us a Son is giv-en, un-to
14
B
p
For un-to us a Child is born,
=
us a Son is giv-en:
p
For un-to
17

un - to
us
a Son is
giv - en,
un - to
us a Child is born,
20
P
WS
EP
49
57
44
us
a Son is
giv - en,
un - to
us
a Son is
un - to us
a Son is giv - en:
23
C
mf
and the gov - ern - ment shall
3
giv-en:
-3
mf
and the gov-ern-ment shall be up-on His shoul - - - - - -
26

cresc.
be up-on His shoul - - - - - - - - der, up-on His shoul-der; and His
mf
cresc.
and the gov-ern-ment shall be up-on His shoul-der; and His
cresc.
- der; and His
mf
cresc.
and the gov-ern-ment shall be up-on His shoul-der; and His
29
50
58
D
ff
Name shall be call-ed Won-der-ful, Coun-sel-lor,
ff
Name shall be call-ed Won-der-ful, Coun-sel-lor,
ff
Name shall be call-ed Won-der-ful, Coun-sel-lor,
ff
Name shall be call-ed Won-der-ful, Coun-sel-lor,
32
45
The Migh-ty God, The Ev-er-last-ing Fa-ther, The Prince of Peace.
p
The Migh-ty God, The Ev-er-last-ing Fa-ther, The Prince of Peace. Un-to
The Migh-ty God, The Ev-er-last-ing Fa-ther, The Prince of Peace.
The Migh-ty God, The Ev-er-last-ing Fa-ther, The Prince of Peace.
35

us a Child is born,
un - to us
a Son is
-4
For un-to us a Child is born,
51
59
Un - to us a Child is born,
giv - en:
and the gov - ern - ment shall
un - to us a Son is giv - en:
be up - on His shoul - - - - -
and the gov - ern - ment shall be up - on His shoul - - -

46
E
cresc.
ff
and His Name shall be call - ed Won - der - ful,
cresc.
ff
- der; and His Name shall be call - ed Won - der - ful,
cresc.
-4
ff
and His Name shall be call-ed Won - der - ful,
=
cresc.
ff
- der; and His Name shall be call - ed Won - der - ful,
47
52
60
Coun - sel - lor, The Migh - ty God, The Ev - er - last - ing Fa - ther, The
Coun - sel - lor, The Migh - ty God, The Ev - er - last - ing Fa - ther, The
-3
Coun-sel-lor, The Migh-ty God, The Ev-er-last-ing Fa-ther, The
Coun - sel - lor, The Migh - ty God, The Ev - er - last - ing Fa - ther, The
50
p
Prince of Peace. For un - to us a Child is born,
Prince of Peace.
p
Prince of Peace. Un - to us a Child is born,
p
Prince of Peace. For un - to
53

E P
47
For un - to us a Child is born,
us a Child is born,
un - to us a Son is
56
P
W S
53
61
un - to us a Son is giv - en:
+4
-2
un-to us a Son is giv-en: and the gov-ern-ment shall
giv - en:
59
and the gov - ern - ment shall be up-on His shoul - - -
be up-on His shoul - - - der;
62

cresc.
- der; and His Name shall be call - ed
mf
cresc.
and the gov - ern - ment shall be up - on His shoul - der; and His Name shall be call - ed
cresc.
and His Name shall be call-ed
mf
cresc.
and the gov - ern - ment shall be up - on His shoul - der; and His Name shall be call - ed
65
48
54
62
F
ff
Won - der - ful, Coun - sel - lor, The Migh - ty God, The
ff
Won - der - ful, Coun - sel - lor, The Migh - ty God, The
ff
Won - der - ful, Coun - sel - lor, The Migh - ty God, The
ff
Won - der - ful, Coun - sel - lor, The Migh - ty God, The
68
f
Ev - er - last - ing Fa - ther, Prince of Peace. For un - to
f
Ev - er - last - ing Fa - ther, Prince of Peace. For un - to
f
+2
Ev - er - last - ing Fa - ther, Prince of Peace. For un - to
f
Ev - er - last - ing Fa - ther, Prince of Peace. Un - to us a Child is born, un - to
71

us a Child is born,
us a Child is born,
us a Child is born, un - to us a Son is
74
us a Child is born, un - to us a Son is
49
55
63
un - to us
un - to us
giv - en, un - to us a Son is giv - en, un - to us
76
giv - en, un - to us a Son is giv - en, un - to us
a Son is giv - en: and the gov - ern - ment, the gov - ern - ment shall
a Son is giv - en: and the gov - ern - ment shall
a Son is giv - en:
79
a Son is giv - en:

be up - on His shoul - - - - der, and the gov - ern - ment shall
be up - on His shoul - der, and the gov - ern - ment shall
=
and the gov - ern - ment, the gov - ern - ment shall
and the gov - ern - ment, the gov - ern - ment shall
81
G
ff
be up - on His shoul - der; and His Name shall be call - ed Won - der - ful,
be up - on His shoul - der; and His Name shall be call - ed Won - der - ful,
be up-on His shoul-der; and His Name shall be call-ed Won-der-ful,
be up - on His shoul - der; and His Name shall be call - ed Won - der - ful,
83
EP P WS
50 56 64
Coun - sel - lor, The Migh - ty God, The Ev - er - last - ing Fa - ther, The
Coun - sel - lor, The Migh - ty God, The Ev - er - last - ing Fa - ther, The
-3
Coun-sel-lor, The Migh-ty God, The Ev-er-last-ing Fa-ther, The
Coun - sel - lor, The Migh - ty God, The Ev - er - last - ing Fa - ther, The
86

13 Pastoral Symphony

14 Recitative – There Were Shepherds Abiding In The Field (Soprano)

There were shepherds abiding in the field
Keeping watch over their flocks by night.

Recitative – And Lo, The Angel Of The Lord Came Upon Them (Soprano)

And lo, the angel of the Lord came upon them
And the glory of the Lord shone round about them
And they were sore afraid.

15 Recitative – And The Angel Said Unto Them (Soprano)

And the angel said unto them:
'Fear not, for behold
I bring you good tidings of great joy
Which shall be to all people.
For unto you is born this day
In the city of David
A Saviour
Which is Christ the Lord.'

16 Recitative – And Suddenly There Was With The Angel (Soprano)

17 Chorus – Glory To God

EP 54 P 61 WS 68

Allegro ♩ = 90

S *mp* Glo - ry to God, glo - ry to God in the high - - - est,

A *mp* Glo - ry to God, glo - ry to God in the high - - - est,

T *mp* Glo-ry to God, glo-ry to God in the high - est, +2

B

orch.

say - ing,

69
-4
and peace on earth,
and peace on earth,
-2
5
A
55
62
Glo - ry to God, glo - ry to God, glo - ry to God in the high - est,
Glo - ry to God, glo - ry to God, glo - ry to God in the high - est,
Glo - ry to God, glo - ry to God, glo - ry to God in the high - est,
+4
10
B
and peace on earth,
+2
good - will
and peace on earth,
good - will to - wards
14

70
f
good - will to - wards men, to - wards men,
f
good - will to - wards men, to - wards men, good - will to - wards
to - wards men, to - wards men,
+2
men, good - will
19
56
63
good - will to - wards men, to - wards
men, to - wards men, good - will to - wards
good - will to - wards men, good - will to - wards
to - wards men, good - will to - wards
22
C
71
ff
men. Glo - ry to God, glo - ry to God in the high - est,
ff
men. Glo - ry to God, glo - ry to God in the high - est,
5
+6
ff 3
men. Glo - ry to God, glo - ry to God in the high - est,
ff
men. Glo - ry to God, glo - ry to God in the high - est,
25

f
and peace on earth,
and peace on earth, good-will to - wards
+2
and peace on earth, good - will
and peace on earth,
29
64
72
57
D
good-will, good-will, good-will,
men, to - - - - wards men, good - will, good - will, good - will,
=
to - wards men, to - wards men, good-will, good-will, good-will,
good - will, good - will, good - will,
34
good - will to - wards men, good - will to -
good - will to - wards men, good - will
good - will to - wards men, good - will
good - will to - wards men, good - will
38

18 Air – Rejoice Greatly, O Daughter Of Zion! (Soprano)

Rejoice greatly, O daughter of Zion!
Shout, O daughter of Jerusalem!
Behold, thy King cometh unto thee.

He is the righteous Saviour
And He shall speak peace unto the heathen.

19 Recitative – Then Shall The Eyes Of The Blind Be Opened (Alto)

Then shall the eyes of the blind be opened
And the ears of the deaf unstopped
Then shall the lame man leap as an hart
And the tongue of the dumb shall sing.

20 Air – He Shall Feed His Flock Like A Shepherd (Alto)

He shall feed His flock like a shepherd
And He shall gather the lambs with His arm
And carry them in His bosom
And gently lead those that are with young.

(Soprano)
Come unto Him, all ye that labour
Come unto Him, ye that are heavy laden
And He will give you rest.

Take His yoke upon you and learn of Him
For He is meek and lowly of heart
And ye shall find rest unto your souls.

21 Chorus – His Yoke Is Easy, And His Burthen Is Light

Allegro ♩ = 82

p

His yoke is ea - - - - - - - sy, His bur - then is

71
yoke is ea - - - - - - - - sy, His bur-then is light,
- sy, His bur-then is light, His bur-then is light, His
His yoke is ea - - - - - -
7
76
87
A
His bur-then is light, His bur-then, His
His bur - then is light,
bur-then, His bur-then, His bur - then is light, is light,
- - sy, His bur - then, His bur - then is light,
10
bur - then is light, His bur-then, His bur - then is light,
His bur - then is light,
His bur-then is light, is light,
His bur-then, His bur - then is light, His yoke is
13

p
His yoke is ea - - - - -
p
His bur - then is
ea - - - - - - - - - - - sy,
16
f
- - - sy, His bur - then is light,
72
p
His
f
light, His bur-then, His bur - then is light,
p
His yoke is ea - - - - - -
f
His bur - then is light,
18
77
88
B
f
yoke is ea - - - - - - - - sy, His bur - then is light,
p
His yoke is
f
- sy, His bur-then is light, His bur-then, His bur - then is light,
f
His bur - then is light His
21

His
ea - - - - - - - - - - - sy, His bur - then is
yoke is ea - - - - - - - - - - - - - - sy,
24
73
bur - then is light,
His bur-then, His bur-then, His bur - then is
light, His bur - then, His bur - then is light, His bur - then is
His bur-then is light,
His
His bur - then, His bur-then, His bur - then, His
27
78
89
C
light, His yoke is ea - - - - - - - sy, His
light,
bur - then, His bur - then is light,
bur - then, His bur - then is light, His yoke is ea - - - - - -
30

f
p
bur - then is light, His bur - then is light,
His bur - then is light, His bur - then is
=
His bur - then is light, is light,
- sy, His bur - then is light, is light,
33
His bur-then, His bur - then, His bur - then, His bur
light, His bur - then is light, His bur - then is light, His bur -
=
-3
His bur - then is light, is light, His bur -
His bur - then is light, is light, His bur -
36
74
79
90
D
then is light, His yoke is
then is light, His yoke is
then is light, His yoke is
then is light, His yoke is
39

ea - - - - - - - - sy, and His bur - then is light, His yoke is
ea - sy, His yoke is ea - sy, His bur - then is light, His yoke is
ea - sy, is ea - - - - sy, His bur-then is light, His yoke is
ea - sy, is ea - - - - - - - sy, His bur - then is light, His yoke is
42

ea - sy, His bur - then is light, His yoke is ea - sy,
ea - sy, His bur - then is light, His yoke is ea - sy,
+3
ea - sy, His bur - then is light, His yoke is ea - sy,
ea - sy, His bur - then is light, His yoke is ea - sy,
45

(p) ff
and His bur - - - - - - - then is light.
(p) ff
and His bur - - - - - - - then is light.
(p) ff
and His bur - - - - then is light.
(p) ff
and His bur - - - - - - - then is light.
48

END OF PART I

Part II

22 Chorus – Behold The Lamb Of God

CD1 Track 8   CD2 Track 53

P 75   P 80   WS 91

Note: All dotted rhythms in this chorus have been standardised in accordance with common performance practice.

76
cresc.
God that ta - keth, that ta - keth a - way the sin of the world,
cresc.
f
that ta - keth a - way the sin of the world, be -
-3
cresc.
f
God that ta - keth a - way the sin of the world, be -
cresc.
f
- hold the Lamb of God that ta - keth a - way the sin of the world,
7

81
92
A
f
be - hold the Lamb of God, the Lamb of God, be -
- hold the Lamb of God, the Lamb of God, be - hold the Lamb of
=
- hold the Lamb of God, be - hold the Lamb of God, be -
be - hold the Lamb of
10

- hold the Lamb of God that ta - keth a - way the sin of the world, of
God, the Lamb of God that ta - keth a - way the sin of the world, the
- hold the Lamb of God that ta - keth a - way the sin of the world, the
God that ta - keth a - way the sin of the world, the
12

B
the world, be - hold the Lamb of God, be - hold the Lamb of God that
sin of the world, be - hold the Lamb of God, the Lamb of God
sin of the world, be - hold the Lamb of God, the Lamb of God
sin of the world, be - hold the Lamb of God, the lamb of God
15
77 82 93
ta - keth a-way the sin of the world,
that ta - keth a - way the sin, the sin of the world, the
-4
that ta - keth a-way the sin of the world, the
that ta - keth a - way the sin of the world, the
18
C
that ta - keth a - way the sin
sin of the world, that ta - keth a - way the
-3
sin of the world, that ta - keth a-
sin of the world, that ta - keth a-
21

of the world, the sin of the
sin, the sin of the world, the sin of the world, the sin of the
-way the sin of the world, the sin of the world, the sin of the
-way the sin of the world, the sin of the world,
24

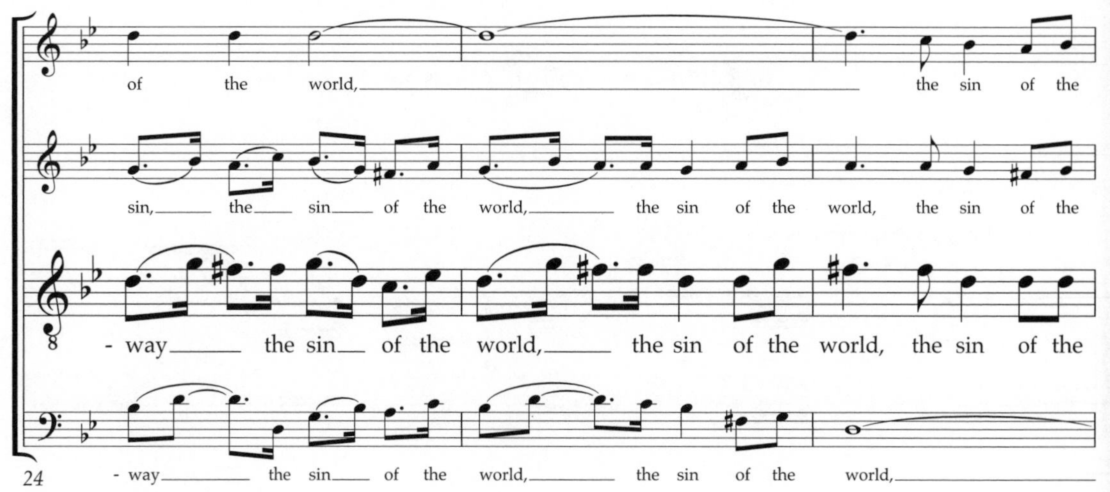

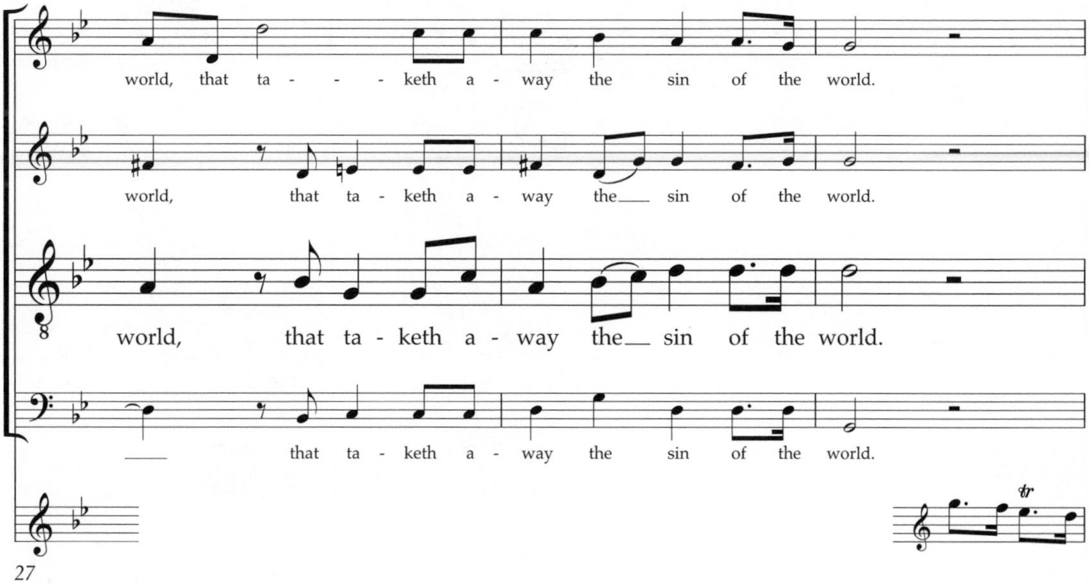

world, that ta - - - keth a - way the sin of the world.
world, that ta - keth a - way the sin of the world.
world, that ta - keth a - way the sin of the world.
that ta - keth a - way the sin of the world.
27

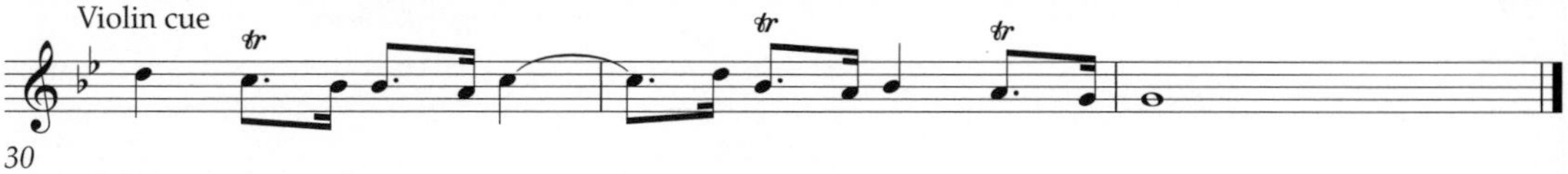

Violin cue
30

23 Air – He Was Despised (Alto)

He was despised and rejected of men
A man of sorrows, and acquainted with grief.

He gave His back to the smiters
And His cheeks to them that plucked off the hair.
He hid not His face from shame and spitting.

24 Chorus – Surely He Hath Borne Our Griefs

CD1 Track 9 CD2 Tracks 54-55

88
99
borne our griefs, and car - ried our sor - rows, sure - ly, sure - ly He hath
7
83
borne our griefs, and car - ried our sor - rows.
He
10
89
100
A
mf
He was wound - ed for our trans - gres - sions, He was bruis - ed,
was wound - ed for our trans - gres - sions, He was bruis - ed,
+2
He was wound - ed for our trans - gres - sions, He was bruis - ed, He
13

REMAIN STANDING

25 Chorus – And With His Stripes We Are Healed

Alla breve – Moderato 𝅗𝅥 = 102

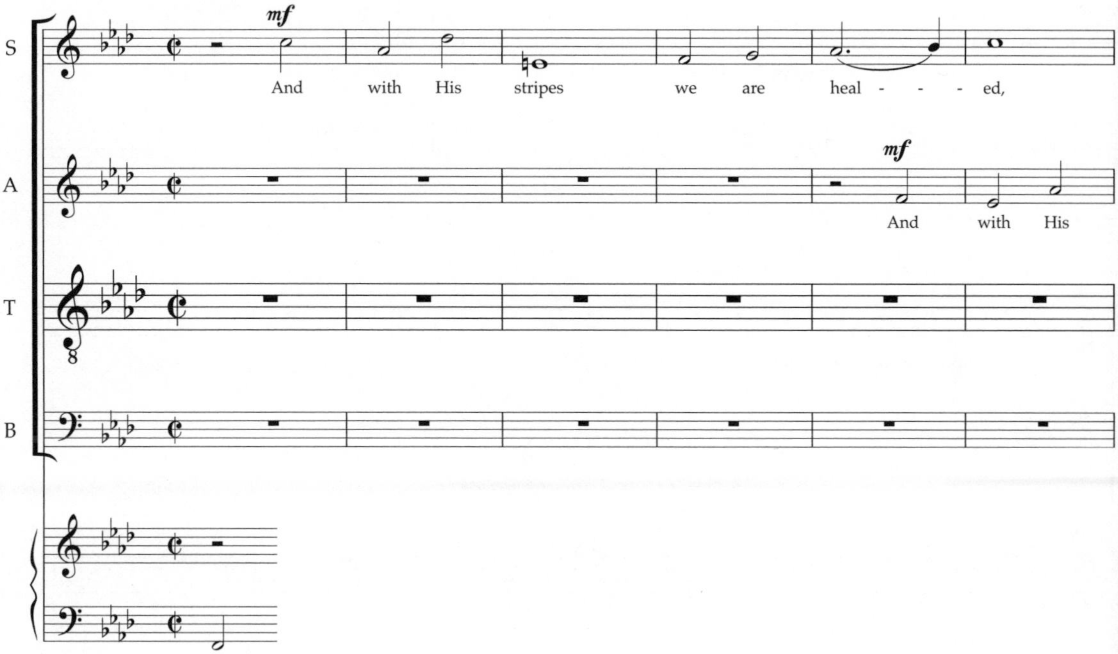

S: *mf* And with His stripes we are heal - - - ed,

A: *mf* And with His

T

B

P
WS
A
A
- ed, we are heal - ed, and with His
- - - - ed, and with His stripes we are heal - - -
-5
mf
-3
And with His stripes we are heal -
12
stripes we are heal - - - - ed, we are heal - - -
=
- - - - - - ed, and with His
mf
And with His stripes
17
P
WS
EP
92
103
86
B
f
- ed, and with His
- ed, and with His stripes we are heal - ed,
stripes we are heal - ed, we are heal - - - -
we are heal - - - - - - - - - - - - - ed,
22

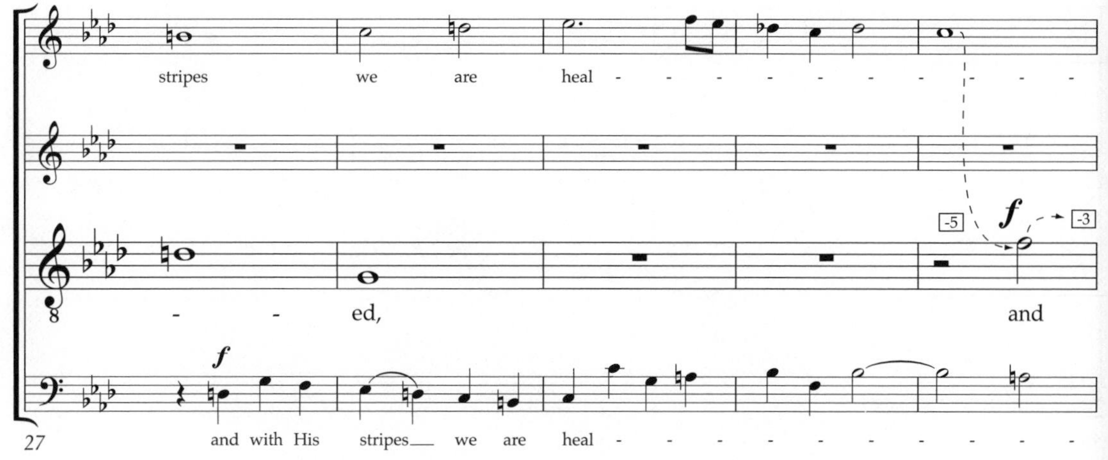
stripes we are heal - - - - - - - - - -
- - ed, and
-5
-3
f
and with His stripes we are heal - - - - - - - - - -
27

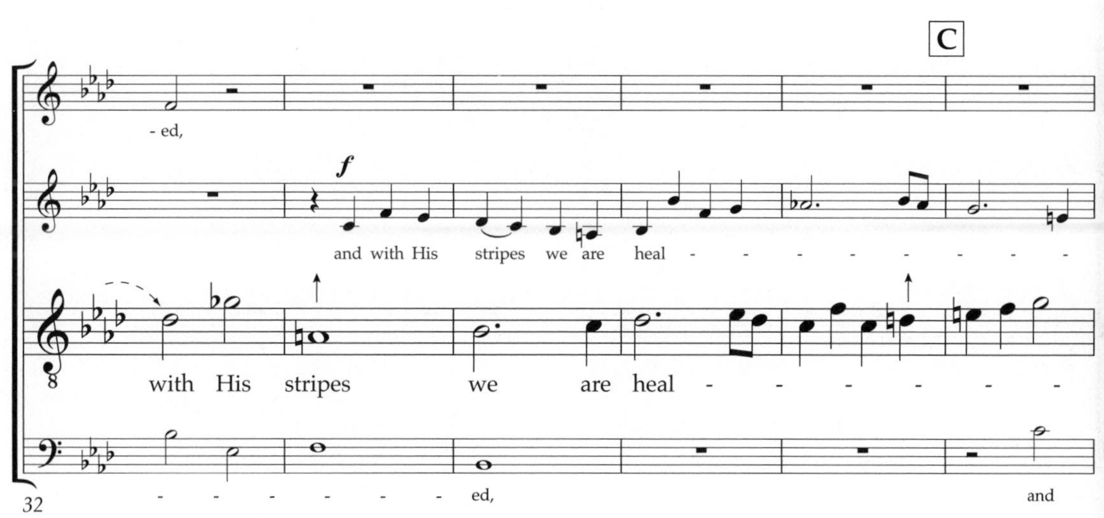
C
- ed,
f
and with His stripes we are heal - - - - - - - -
with His stripes we are heal - - - - - - -
- - - - - - - ed, and
32

and with His stripes we are heal - - - - - -
- - - - - - - ed,
with His stripes we are heal - - - - - -
38

93
104
87
ed,
and
ed,
43
with His stripes we are heal
ed, are heal
and with his stripes we are heal
49
D
and with His stripes we are
ed,
ed,
+5
and with His stripes we are
ed,
54

heal - - - - - - - - - - - - ed, and
and with His stripes we are
heal - - - - - - - - - - ed,
and with His stripes we are heal - - - - ed,
59
E
94
88
105
with his stripes we are heal - - - - - ed,
heal - ed,
and with his
and with His stripes we are heal - - - - - -
and with His stripes
64
stripes we are heal - - - - - - - - - - - - - - -
- - ed, and with His stripes we
we are heal - - - - - - - - - - - - - - ed,
70

REMAIN STANDING

26 Chorus – All We Like Sheep Have Gone Astray

EP 89 P 95 WS 106

Allegro moderato ♩ = 102

S: All we like sheep, all we like sheep have gone a - stray

A: All we like sheep, all we like sheep,

T: All we like sheep, all we like sheep have gone a - stray,

B: All we like sheep, all we like sheep,

5

S: all we like sheep, all we like

A: all we like sheep, all we like

T: all we like sheep, all we like

B: all we like sheep, all we like

A
sheep;
we have turn - - - - -
sheep have gone a - stray;
+3
sheep;
we have
sheep have gone a - stray;
9
P 96
WS 107
EP 90
- - - - - - - ed ev - 'ry one to his own way,
we have turn - - - - - - - - - -
turn - ed
12
- ed ev - 'ry one to his own way, ev - 'ry one to his own way,
all we like
all we like
=
ev - 'ry one to his own way,
all we like
all we like
15

sheep
have gone a - stray;
sheep
have gone a - stray;
sheep
have gone a - stray;
sheep
have gone a - stray;
18
B
97
108
we have turn - ed,
(f)
we have turn - - - - - - - - -
22
91
we have turn - - - - - - - - - - ed ev - 'ry one to
we have turn - ed, we have
- ed ev - 'ry one to his own way,
we have turn - ed ev - 'ry
we have
25

C
his own way, to his own way, we have turn - ed
turn - ed ev - 'ry one to his own way, we have
one to his own way, we have turn - ed
turn - ed ev - 'ry one to his own way,
28
98
109
(p)
ev - 'ry one to his own way, all
turn - ed ev - 'ry one to his own way, all
ev - 'ry one to his own way, all
we have turn - ed ev - 'ry one to his own way, all
31
we like sheep have gone a - stray,
we like sheep have gone a - stray,
we like sheep have
we like sheep
34

92
D
have gone a - stray;
gone a-stray;
we have
have gone a - stray;
38

99
110
we have turn - ed
ev - 'ry one to his own
turn - ed,
we have turn
42

we have turn - ed, we have turn-ed ev - 'ry one to
way, we have turn - ed ev - 'ry one to
-6
we have turn-ed, we have turn-ed ev-'ry one to
ed, we have turn - ed, we have turn-ed ev - 'ry one to
45

93
his own way, we have turn-ed ev-'ry
his own way, we have turn-ed ev-'ry one to his own way,
his own way, we have turn-ed ev-'ry one to his own way,
his own way, we have turn-ed ev-'ry one, ev-'ry one to his own
48
E
100
111
(p)
one to his own way, to his own way, all we like sheep, all
ev-'ry one to his own way, all we like sheep, all
we have turn-ed ev-'ry one to his own way, all we like sheep, all
way, ev-'ry one to his own way, all we like sheep, all
-3
51
mp
have gone a-stray;
we like sheep have gone a-stray;
we like sheep have gone a-stray;
mp mf
we like sheep have gone a-stray:
we like sheep have gone a-stray;
55

94
we have turn-ed,
we have turn-ed
we have turn-ed,
+2
we have turn-ed, we have
59
we have turn-ed,
we have turn-ed
101
112
F
ev - 'ry one to his own way,
we have turn - ed
ev - 'ry one to his own way,
we have
turn - ed
-2
ev - 'ry one to his own way,
ev - 'ry one to his own way, we have turn - - -
63
we have turn - - - - ed,
we have
turn - - - ed, we have turn - ed,
we have turn - - - - ed, we have
=
we have turn - - - - ed
66
- ed, we have turn - ed,
we have turn - - -

95
turn - - - - - - - - - - - - - ed, we have
turn - - - - - - - - - - - - - ed, we have turn-ed
+5
ev-'ry one to his own way, we have turn-ed
- - ed ev - 'ry one to his own way, we have
69
102
113
(cresc.)
(ff)
turn - ed ev - 'ry one to his own way, we have turn - ed ev - 'ry one to his own
ev - 'ry one to his own way, we have turn - ed ev - 'ry one to his own
ev-'ry one to his own way, we have turn-ed ev-'ry one to his own
turn - ed ev - 'ry one to his own way, we have turn - ed ev - 'ry one to his own
72
G
Adagio ♩ = 52
mf
cresc.
way, and the Lord hath laid on Him, and the
way, and the Lord hath
-6
way, and the Lord hath laid on
(ff) mf
(mf)
way, and the Lord hath laid on Him,
76

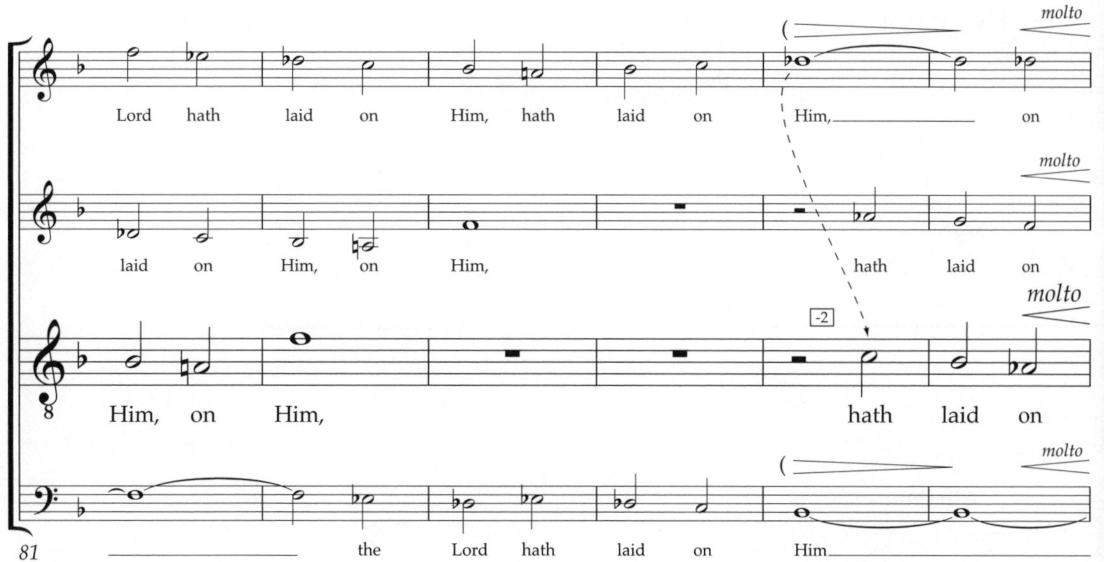

REMAIN STANDING through

27 Recitative – All They That See Him, Laugh Him To Scorn (Tenor)

All they that see Him, laugh Him to scorn
They shoot out their lips
And shake their heads, saying:

28 Chorus – He Trusted In God That He Would Deliver Him

CD1 Track 12 CD2 Tracks 63-66

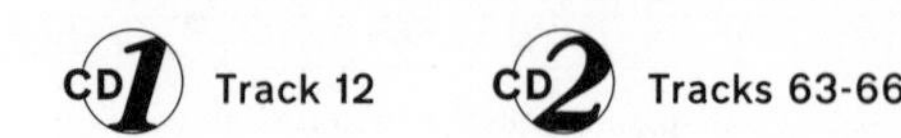

Tenor cue
Larghetto
and shake their heads, say - ing:

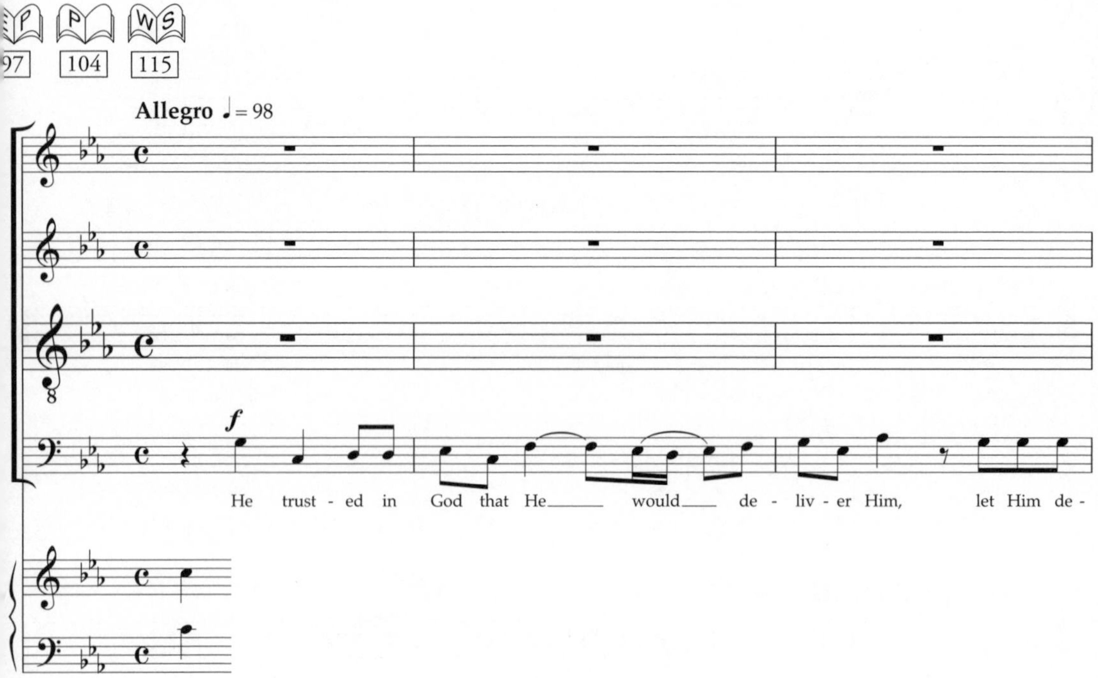

97
104
115
Allegro ♩= 98
f
He trust - ed in God that He would de - liv - er Him, let Him de -

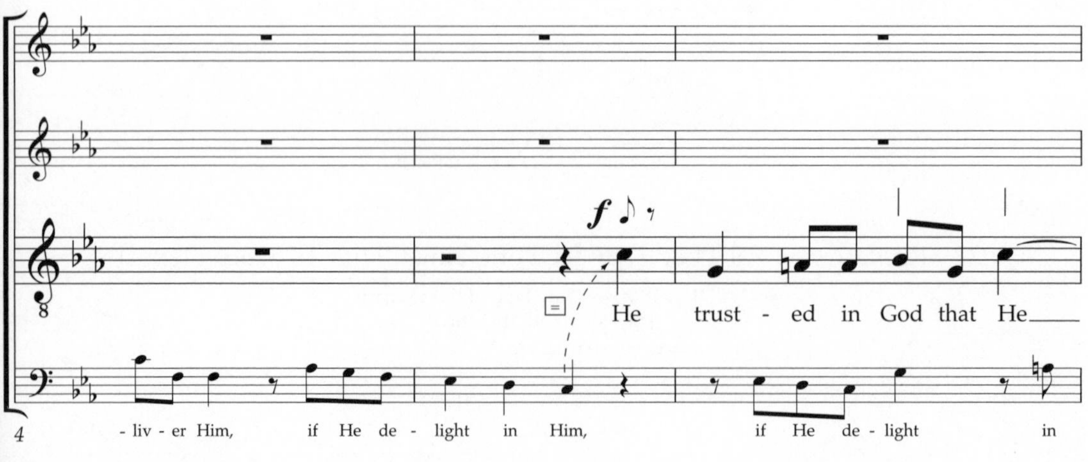

f
He trust - ed in God that He
4
- liv - er Him, if He de - light in Him, if He de - light in

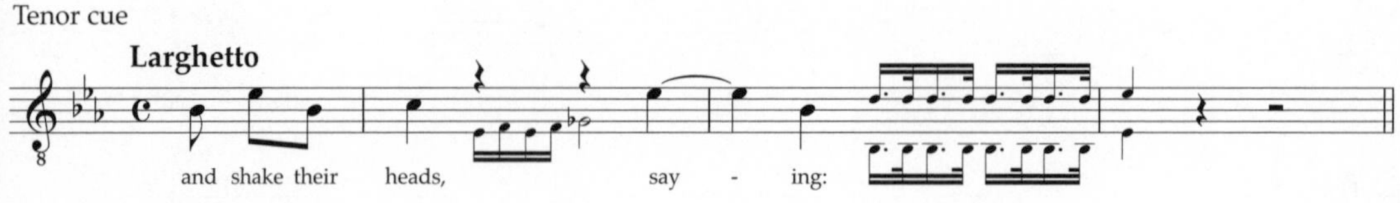

would de-liv-er Him, let Him de-liv-er Him, if He de-light in
7
Him, let him de-liv-er Him, if He de-light in Him, if He de-light in
A
105
116
He trust-ed in God that He would de-liv-er Him, let him de-
Him, if He de-light in Him, let Him de-liv-er Him, if He de-
10
Him, if He de-light in Him,
98
He trust-ed in God that He
-liv-er Him, if He de-light in Him, if He de-light
-light in Him, if He de-light in Him, if He de-light
13
He trust-ed in God, in God, in God He

would de - liv - er Him, let Him de - liv - er Him, if He de - light in
in
in Him,
16
trust - ed, let Him de - liv - er Him, if He de - light in Him, if He de -
106
117
Him, let Him de - liv - er Him, if He de - light
Him, let Him de - liv - er Him, if He de -
let Him de - liv - er Him, if He de - light
19
- light in Him, let Him de - liv - er Him,
B
99
in Him,
- light in Him, He trust - ed in God that He would de -
in Him, if He de - light in Him, let Him de -
22
He trust - ed in God, He trust - ed in God, let Him de - liv - er Him,

f
let Him de - liv - er Him,
- liv - er Him, let Him de - liv - er Him, if He de - light in Him, if He de -
- liv - er Him, if He de - light in Him, if He de - light in Him, He
if He de - light in Him, if He de - light in Him,
25
107
118
He trust - ed in God that He would de - liv - er Him,
- light in Him, let Him de - liv - er Him, if
trust - ed in God, He trust - ed in God, let Him de - liv - er Him, if
28
C
let him de - liv - er Him, if He de - light in Him,
mf
He de - light in Him, if He de - light in Him, let Him de -
mf
He de - light in Him, if He de - light in Him, let Him de - liv - er Him,
f
let Him de - liv - er Him,
31

100
mf
let Him de - liv - er Him,
if He de - light in
- liv - er Him,
let Him de - liv - er Him,
if He de -
He trust - ed in God that He
mf
let Him de - liv - er Him,
34
108
119
Him,
if He de - light in Him,
let Him de - liv - er Him,
- light in Him,
let Him de -
would de-liv - er Him,
let Him de - liv - er Him,
let Him de - liv - er Him,
37
D
if He de - light in Him, let Him de - liv - er Him,
- liv - er Him,
if He de - light in Him,
f
He trust - ed in God, let Him de -
f
if He de - light in Him, let Him de - liv - er him, He trust-ed in God, let Him de -
f
He trust - ed in God, that He
40

EP
101
mf
let Him de-
- liv - er Him, if He de - light in
- liv - er Him, if He de-light in
would de - liv - er Him, let Him de - liv - er Him, if He de-light in
43
P
109
WS
120
- liv - er Him, let Him de-liv - er Him, let Him de-liv - er Him,
mf
Him, let Him de-liv - er Him, if He de-
mf
Him, let Him de - liv - er Him,
mf
Him, let Him de - liv - er Him,
46
E
f
He trust - ed in God that He would de-
f
- light in Him, He trust - ed in God, let Him de - liv - er
+3
f
if He de-light in Him, if He de-light,
f
if He de-light in Him, if He de - light
49

EP
102
- liv - er Him, let Him de - liv - er Him, if He de - light in Him,
Him, if He de - light in Him, let Him de - liv - er Him, let Him de-
if He de - light in Him,
in Him, if He de - light in Him, let Him de-liv - er Him,
52
P
110
WS
121
if He de - light in Him, if He de-
- liv - er Him, if He de - light
let Him de-liv-er Him, if He de-light in Him, if He de-light
He trust - ed in
55
- light in Him, let Him de - liv - er Him,
in Him, let Him de - liv - er Him,
in Him, let Him, let Him de-liv-er Him,
God, that He would de - liv - er Him, let Him, let Him de - liv - er Him,
58

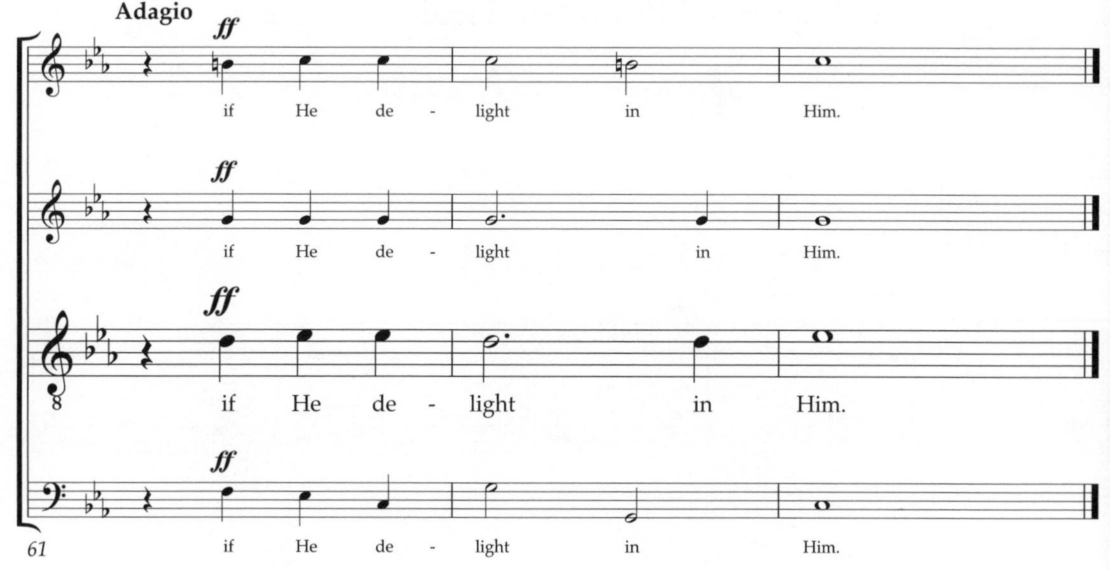

29 Recitative – Thy Rebuke Hath Broken His Heart (Tenor)

Thy rebuke hath broken his heart
He is full of heaviness.
He looked for some to have pity on Him
But there was no man
Neither found He any to comfort Him.

30 Air – Behold, And See If There Be Any Sorrow (Tenor)

Behold, and see, if there be any sorrow
Like unto His sorrow.

31 Recitative – He Was Cut Off Out Of The Land Of The Living (Tenor)

He was cut off out of the land of the living
For the transgression of Thy people
Was He stricken.

32 Air – But Thou Didst Not Leave His Soul In Hell (Tenor)

But Thou didst not leave His soul in hell
Nor didst Thou suffer Thy Holy One to see corruption.

33 Chorus – Lift Up Your Heads, O Ye Gates

mf
Lift up your heads, O ye__ gates, and be ye lift up, ye

mf
Lift up your heads, O ye__ gates, and be ye lift up, ye

mf
Lift up your heads, O ye__ gates, and be ye lift up, ye

4

108
ev - er - last - ing doors, and the King of Glo - ry shall come in.
ev - er - last - ing doors, and the King of Glo - ry shall come in.
ev - er - last - ing doors, and the King of Glo - ry shall come in.
mf
Who
mf
Who
8
A
117
128
is this King of Glo - ry? This King of Glo - ry? Who
is this King of Glo - ry? This King of Glo - ry? Who
+3
11

mf
The Lord strong and might-y, the

mf
The Lord strong and might-y, the

The Lord strong and might-y, the

is this King of Glo-ry? Who is this King of Glo-ry?

is this King of Glo - ry? Who is this King of Glo - ry?

14

109

B

118

Lord strong and might - y, the Lord might - y in bat - tle.

Lord strong and might - y, the Lord might - y in bat - tle.

Lord strong and might - y, the Lord might - y in bat - tle. mf Lift up your heads,

mf
Lift up your heads,

mf
Lift up your heads,

17

O ye gates, and be ye lift up, ye ev - er - last - ing doors, and the
O ye gates, and be ye lift up, ye ev - er - last - ing doors, and the
O ye gates, and be ye lift up, ye ev - er - last - ing doors, and the
20
129
110
King of Glo - ry shall come in, and the King of Glo - ry shall come
King of Glo - ry shall come in, and the King of Glo - ry shall come
-3
King of Glo - ry shall come in, and the King of Glo - ry shall come
23

119
Who is this King of Glo - ry? Who is this King of Glo - ry? Who is this King of Glo - ry? Who
in.
Who is this King of Glo - ry? Who is this King of Glo - ry? Who
in.
in.
26
111
is this King of Glo - ry?
The
The Lord of Hosts,
the
-3
The Lord of Hosts,
+3
the
29

C
120
130
S1
S2
A
T
B
Lord of Hosts, He is the King of Glo - ry, He
Lord of Hosts, He is the King of Glo - ry, He
+2
Lord of Hosts, He is the King of Glo - ry, He
Lord of Hosts, He is the King of Glo - ry, He
32
is the King of Glo - ry, He is the King of Glo - ry, He is the King of
is the King of Glo - ry, He is the King of Glo - ry, He is the King of Glo - ry, He
is the King of Glo-ry, He is the King of Glo-ry, He is the King of Glo - ry, He
is the King of Glo - ry, He is the King of Glo - ry,
35
Glo - ry, He is the King of Glo-ry, He is the King of Glo -
is the King of Glo - ry, the Lord of Hosts, He is the King of Glo -
=
is the King of Glo-ry, the Lord of Hosts, He is the King of Glo -
the Lord of Hosts, He is the King of Glo -
38

112
D
- - - - - - ry, the Lord of Hosts, He is the King of Glo - - -
- - - - - - ry, the Lord of Hosts, He is the King of
=
- ry, the Lord of Hosts, He is the King of
- - - - - - - - ry,
41
121
131
- - - - - - - - - - - - - - - - - - - ry,
Glo - - - - - - - - - - - - - ry, of Glo - - ry, the Lord of
Glo - - - - - - - - - - - - - ry,
44
the Lord of Hosts, He is the King of Glo - - -
Hosts, He is the King of Glo - - - - - ry, of Glo - - -
+3
the Lord of Hosts, He is the King of Glo - ry, of Glo - - -
the Lord of Hosts, He is the King of Glo - - - ry, of Glo - - -
47

50
- - - - - - - - - - - - - - - - ry, He
- - - - - - - - - - - - - - - - ry, He
- - ry, of Glo - - - - - - ry, He
- - - - - - - - - - - - - - - - ry, He
113
E
is the King of Glo - ry, He is the King of Glo - ry, the Lord of Hosts,
is the King of Glo - ry, He is the King of Glo - ry, the Lord of
+3
is the_ King of Glo-ry, He is the_ King of Glo-ry, the Lord of
is the_ King of Glo - ry, He is the_ King of Glo - ry, the Lord of
53
122
132
the Lord of Hosts, the Lord of Hosts, the Lord of Hosts, He
Hosts, the Lord of Hosts, the Lord of Hosts, the Lord of
=
=
=
Hosts, the Lord of Hosts, the Lord of Hosts, the Lord of
Hosts, the Lord of Hosts, the Lord of Hosts, the Lord of
56

is the King of Glo - - - - - - - - - - - - - - - - - -
Hosts, He is the King of Glo - - - - - - - ry, of
Hosts, He is the King of Glo - - - - ry, of
Hosts, He is the King of Glo - - - - - - - - - - - - - - -
59
114
- - ry, He is the King of Glo - ry, He is the King of Glo - ry,
Glo - ry, He is the King of Glo - ry, He is the King of Glo - ry,
Glo - ry, He is the King of Glo - ry, He is the King of Glo - ry,
- - ry, He is the King of Glo - ry, He is the King of Glo - ry,
62
F
123
133
cresc.
the Lord of Hosts, the Lord of Hosts, the Lord of
cresc.
the Lord of Hosts, the Lord of Hosts, the Lord of Hosts, He
-4
cresc.
=
the Lord of Hosts, the Lord of Hosts, the Lord of Hosts, He
cresc.
the Lord of Hosts, the Lord of Hosts, the Lord of
65

REMAIN STANDING through

34 Recitative – Unto Which Of The Angels Said He At Any Time (Tenor)

Unto which of the angels said He at any time
Thou art my Son, this day have I begotten Thee?

35 Chorus – Let All The Angels Of God Worship Him

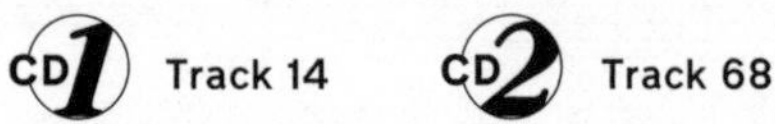

Tenor cue

Allegro

Thou art My Son, this day have I be - got - ten Thee?

15 124 134

Allegro ♩= 96

Let all the an - gels of God wor - - - ship

Let all the an - gels of God wor - - - - ship

Let all the an - gels of God wor - - - - ship

Let all the an - gels of God wor - - - - ship

116
Him,
let all the an - gels of
Him,
let all the an - - - - - - gels of
Him,
Him,
4
125
135
God, let all the an - - - - - - - - - gels of God wor - ship
God wor - - - - - - - - - - - - - - - - ship
let all the an - gels of God wor - - - - - - - ship
7
A
Him,
let all the an - - - - gels of
Him, let all the an - gels of God wor - ship Him,
-4
let all the an - - - - gels of God wor - - - -
10
Him,
let all the an - gels of

God wor - - - ship Him, let all the an - - -
- - - - - - - - ship Him, let all the
God wor - - - - - - - - - - - ship Him,
13
117
126
136
- - - - gels of God wor - ship Him,
let all the an - gels of God wor - - - -
an - gels of God wor - ship Him,
let all the an - - - - - - - - - - - - -
16
- - ship Him, let all the an - - - - gels of
-4
let all the an - - - - - gels of God wor - ship Him,
- gels of God wor - - - - - - - - - - - - ship
19

B
let all the an - - - - - - - - - - - gels of God wor -
God wor - - - - - - ship Him, wor - - - - - - -
let all the an - gels of God wor - - - - -
Him,
22
P
127
WS
137
- - - - - - - - - - - - - - - ship Him, let
- - - - - - - - - - - - - - ship Him, let all the
- - - - - - ship Him, let all the an -
let all the
25
EP
118
C
all the an - - - - - - gels of God, let all the an - gels of
an - - - - - - - - - gels of God, let all the an - gels of
- - - - - - gels of God, let all the an - gels of
an -
28

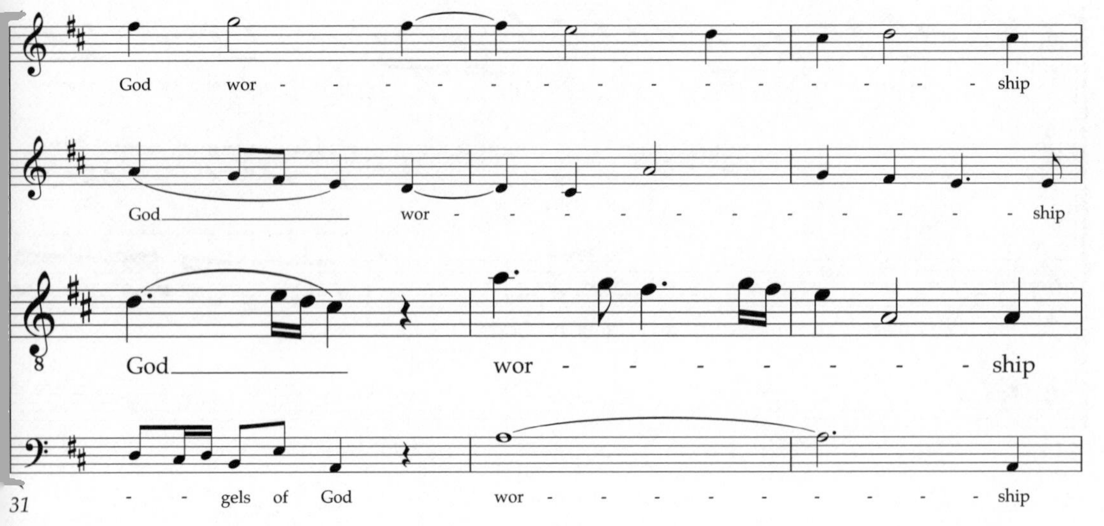

36 Air – Thou Art Gone Up On High (Bass)

Thou art gone up on high
Thou hast led captivity captive
And received gifts for men
Yea, even for Thine enemies
That the Lord God might dwell among them.

37 Chorus – The Lord Gave The Word

EP 122 P 133 WS 146

Andante allegro ♩ = 84

S *f* Great was the com - pa - ny of the

A *f* Great was the com - pa - ny of the

T *f* The Lord gave the word; *f* great was the com - pa - ny of the

B *f* The Lord gave the word; *f* great was the com - pa - ny of the

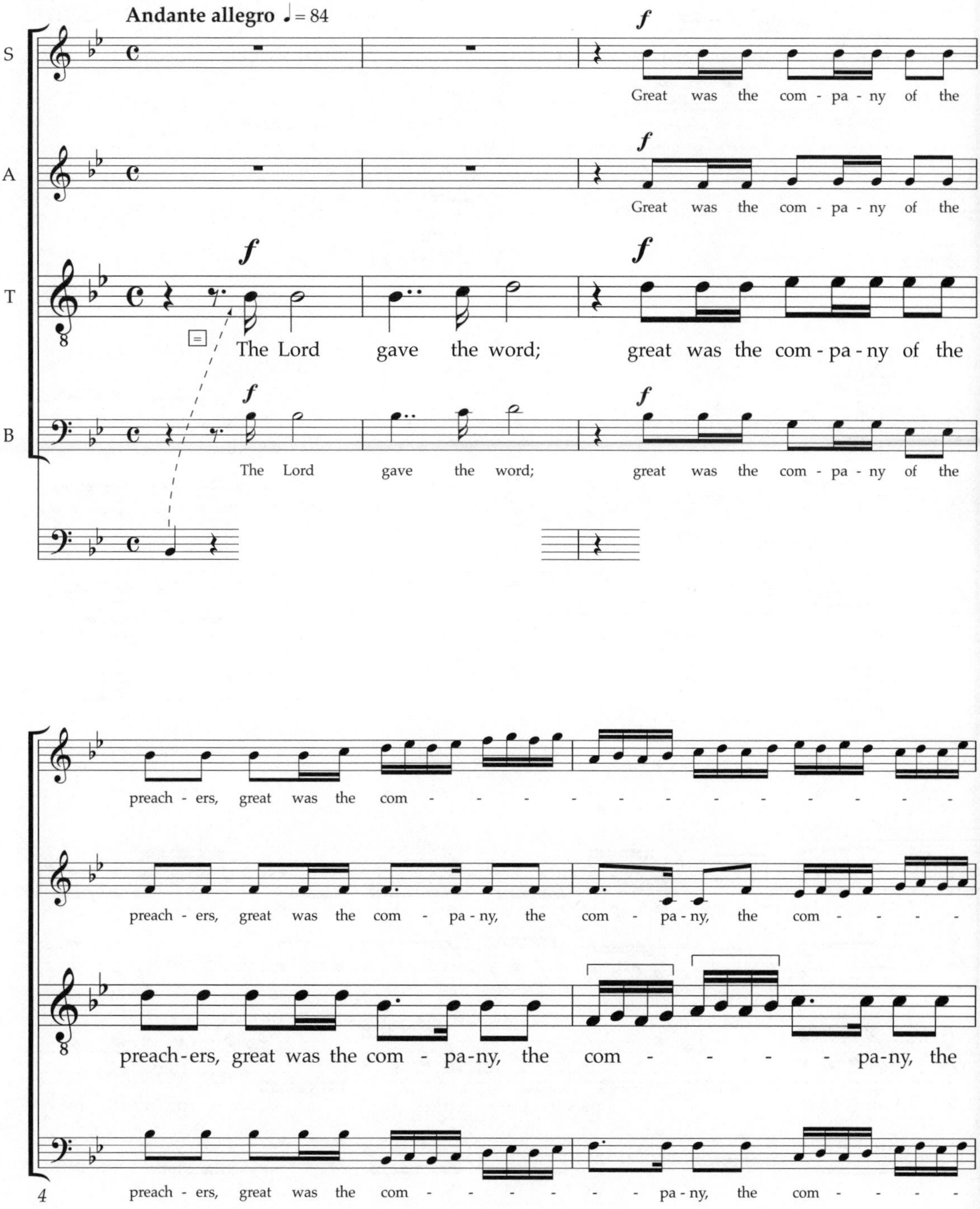

EP
123
- - - - pa-ny of the preach-ers, great was the com-pa-ny of the
- pa-ny, the com-pa-ny of the preach-ers, great was the com-pa-ny of the
=
com - - - pa-ny of the preach-ers, great was the com-pa-ny of the
- - - - pa-ny of the preach-ers, great was the com-pa-ny of the
6
WS
4
147
A
preach-ers. The Lord gave the word; great was the com - - - - -
preach-ers. The Lord gave the word; great was the com - - - -
-3
preach-ers. great was the com - pa-ny, the
preach-ers. great was the com - pa-ny, the
9
- - pa-ny, the com - - - - - - pa-ny, the com - - - -
- - pa-ny, the com - - - - - - pa-ny, the com-pa-ny of the
com - - - - pa-ny, the com - - - - pa-ny of the
com - - - - - - - pa-ny, the com - - - - - - - - -
12

B
- pa - ny of the preach - ers, great was the com - pa - ny of the preach - ers,
preach - ers, of the preach - ers, great was the com - - - - - - - -
preach - ers, of the preach - ers, great was the com - pa - ny of the preach - ers,
- pa - ny of the preach - ers, great was the com - pa - ny, the com - - - -
14
135
148
124
great was the com - pa - ny of the preach - ers, of the preach - ers,
- pa - ny, the com - - - - - - - - - - - - - pa - ny, the
great was the com - pa - ny of the preach - ers, the com - - -
- - - - - - - pa - ny, the com - - - - - - - - - - -
17
great was the com - - - - - - - - - - - - - - -
com - - - - - - - pa - ny, the com - pa - ny, the com - - - -
- - - - - - pa - ny, the com - - - - - pa - ny, the
- - pa - ny, the com - - - - - - - pa - ny, the com - - - -
19

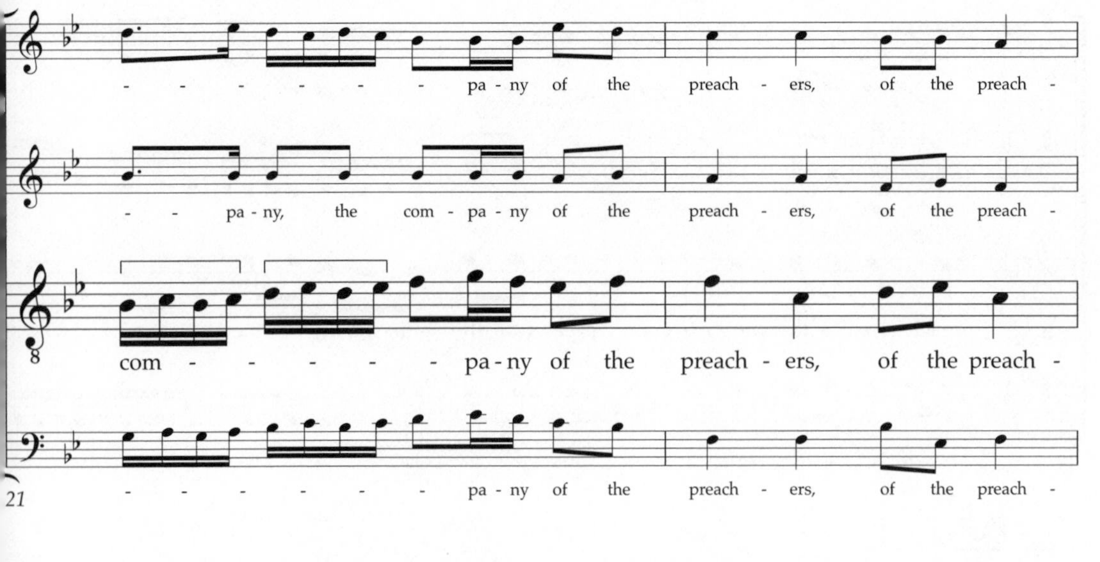

REMAIN STANDING through

38 Air – How Beautiful Are The Feet (Soprano)

How beautiful are the feet of them
That preach the gospel of peace
And bring glad tidings of good things!

39 Chorus – Their Sound Is Gone Out Into All Lands

A tempo ordinario ♩ = 100

S *f* Their sound is gone out in - to all lands, their sound is gone

A *f* Their sound is gone out, in - to all lands,

T *f* Their sound is gone out, their

B *f* Their sound is gone out,

139
152
out in - to all lands, their sound is gone out in - to all
out, is gone out, their sound is gone out, is gone out in - to all
in - to all lands, in - to all lands, in - to all
in - to all lands, their sound is gone out in - to all
8
A
128
lands, and their
lands,
lands, and their words un-to the ends of the world,
lands,
12
words un - to the ends of the world, un - to the
un - to the ends of the world, un - to the
and their words un - to the ends of the
16

140
153
ends of the world,
un-to the
and their words un-to the ends of the world,
un-
ends of the world,
un-to the ends of the
world,
and their words, and their words
un-to the
19
B
ends of the world, their sound is gone out,
is gone out in-to all
-to the ends of the world, their sound is gone out,
is gone out in-to all
+3
world, of the world, their sound is gone out
in-to all
ends of the world,
their sound is gone out in-to all
22
129
lands, and their words un-to the ends of the world,
lands, and their words un-to the ends of the world,
lands, and their words, and their words un-to the ends of the world, of the
lands,
and their words un-to the ends of the
26

40 Air – Why Do The Nations So Furiously Rage Together (Bass)

Why do the nations so furiously rage together?
Why do the people imagine a vain thing?

The kings of the earth rise up
And the rulers take counsel together
Against the Lord
And against his anointed.

40 Air – Why Do The Nations So Furiously Rage Together

CD 1 Track 17

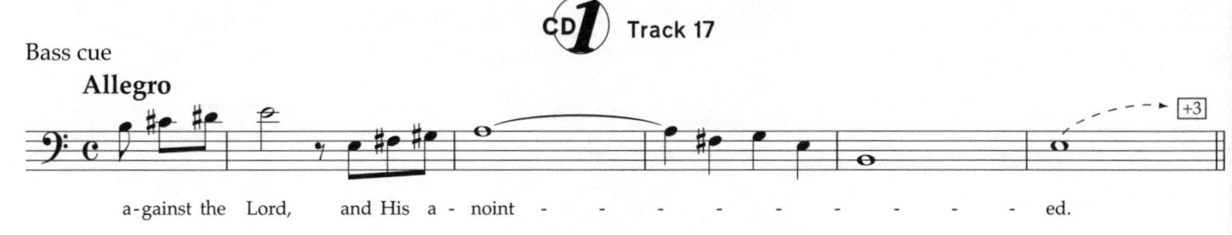

(Two bars click leads straight into:)

41 Chorus – Let Us Break Their Bonds Asunder

CD 1 Track 18 CD 2 Track 73

EP 132 P 148 WS 161

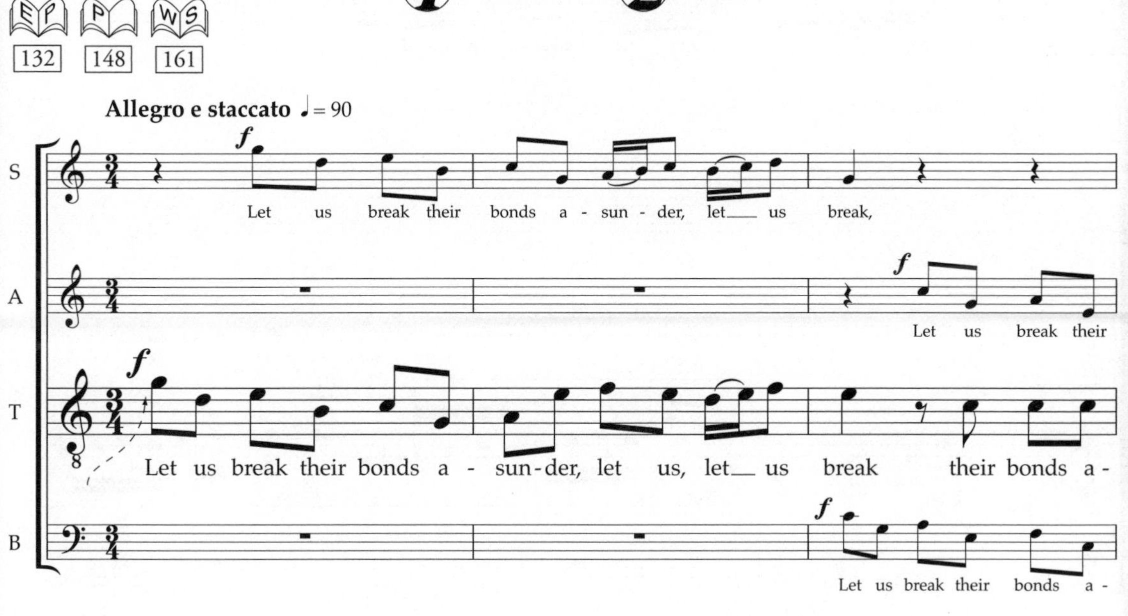

EP 133

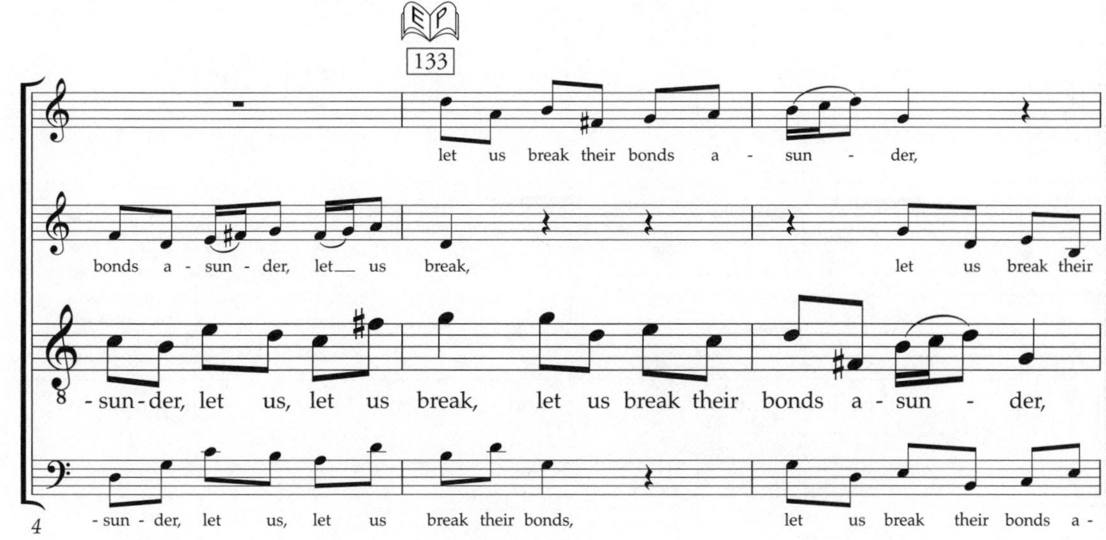

149
162
let us break their bonds a - sun - der,
bonds a - sun - der, let us break their bonds a - sun - der,
-3
let us break their bonds a - sun - der,
- sun - der, let us, let us break their bonds a - sun - der,
7

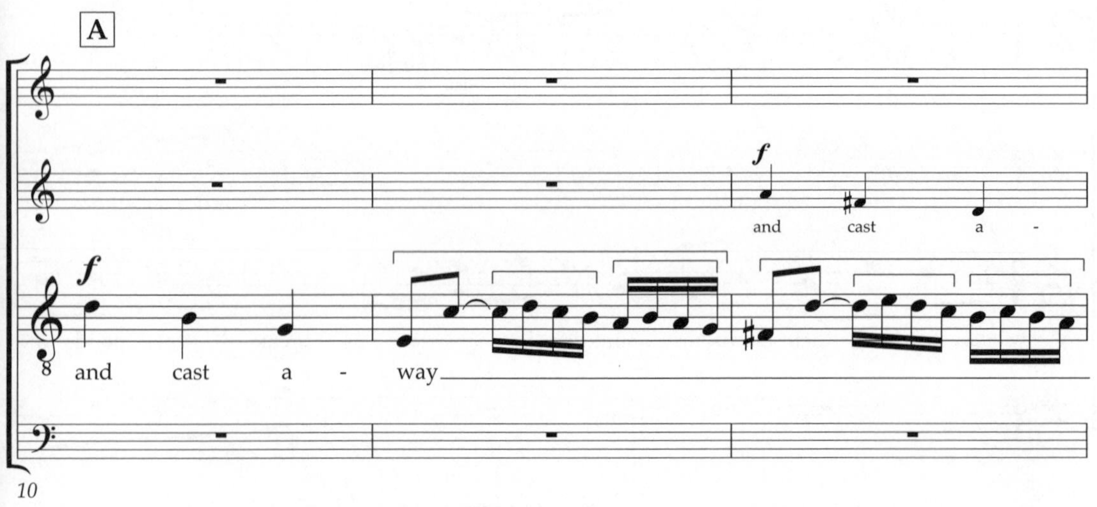
A
f
and cast a -
f
and cast a - way
10

f
and cast a -
- way their yokes from
their yokes from us, and cast a - way their yokes from
13

134
- way their yokes from
us, and cast a - way their yokes from us, and cast a -
us, and cast a - way their yokes from us, and cast a -
and cast a -
16
150
163
us, and cast a - way their yokes from us, and cast a -
- way, and cast a - way their yokes from us, and cast a -
- way, and cast a - way their yokes from us, and cast a -
19 - way, and cast a -
B
- way their yokes from us, let us break their bonds, let us break their
- way their yokes from us, let us break their bonds a -
- way their yokes from us, let us break their bonds,
22 - way their yokes from us,

bonds, let us break their bonds a -
- sun - der, let us break their bonds,
let us break their bonds a - sun - der, let us break their
let us break their bonds a - sun - der, let us break their bonds,
25
135
151
164
- sun - der, let us break their bonds a - sun - der, let us, let us
let us break their bonds a - sun - der,
bonds, let us break their bonds a - sun - der, let us
let us break their bonds a - sun - der
28
break, let us break their bonds a - sun - der, their bonds a -
let us break their bonds, let us break their bonds, their bonds a -
+4
break, let us break their bonds, let us break their bonds a -
let us break their bonds a - sun - der, let us break their bonds a -
31

C
- sun - der, and cast a - way
- sun - der,
- sun - der, and cast a - way,
- sun - der,
34
their yokes from us, and cast a -
and cast a -
and cast a - way, and cast a -
and cast a - - way their
38
136
165
152
- way their yokes from us, and cast a - way their yokes
- way their yokes
- way their yokes from us, and cast a - way their yokes
yokes, their yokes from us, and cast a - way their yokes
41

from us, let us break their bonds a -
from us, let us break their
from us, let us break their bonds a - sun - der,
from us, let us break their bonds,
44
ff
- sun - der, and cast a - - - way,
bonds, and cast a - way their
and cast, and cast a - way, and cast a -
and cast a - way their yokes from us, and cast a -
47
166
and cast a -
yokes, their yokes from us, and cast a - way, and cast a -
- way their yokes from us, and cast a - way, and cast a -
- way their yokes from us, and cast a - way, and cast a -
50

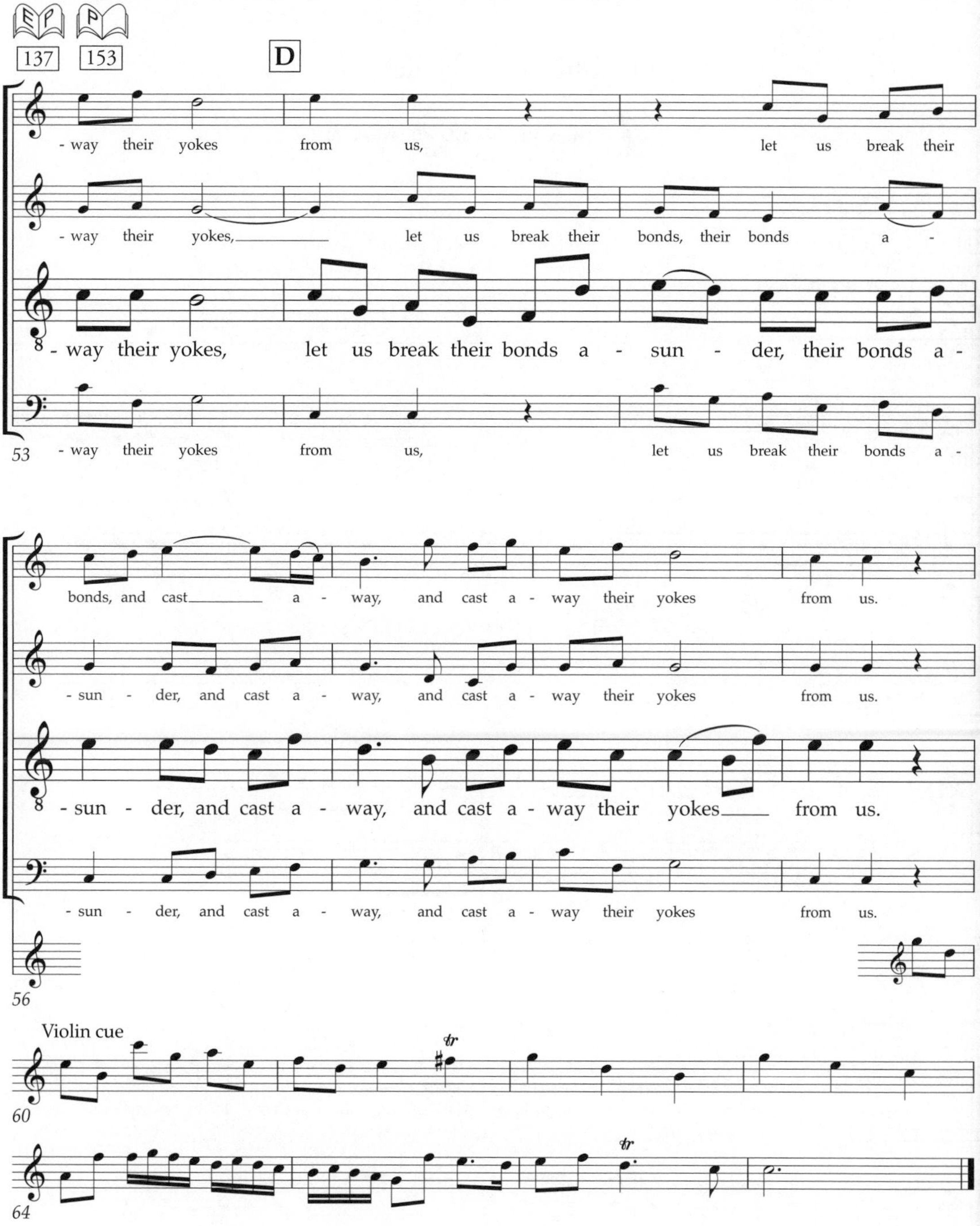

bonds, and cast a - way, and cast a - way their yokes from us.

- sun - der, and cast a - way, and cast a - way their yokes from us.

- sun - der, and cast a - way, and cast a - way their yokes from us.

- sun - der, and cast a - way, and cast a - way their yokes from us.

56

Violin cue

tr

60

tr

64

42 Recitative – He That Dwelleth In Heaven (Tenor)

He that dwelleth in heaven
Shall laugh them to scorn
The Lord shall have them in derision.

43 Air – Thou Shalt Break Them (Tenor)

Thou shalt break them
With a rod of iron.
Thou shalt dash them in pieces
Like a potter's vessel.

44 Chorus – Hallelujah!

41 158 171

Allegro ♩ = 94

Hal - le - lu - jah,

Hal - le - lu - jah,

+2 Hal - le - lu - jah,

Hal - le - lu - jah,

Hal - le - lu - jah, Hal - le - lu - jah, Hal - le - lu - jah, Hal - le - lu - jah,

Hal - le - lu - jah, Hal - le - lu - jah, Hal - le - lu - jah, Hal - le - lu - jah,

Hal - le - lu - jah, Hal - le - lu - jah, Hal - le - lu - jah, Hal - le - lu - jah,

5 Hal - le - lu - jah, Hal - le - lu - jah, Hal - le - lu - jah, Hal - le - lu - jah,

Hal - le - lu - jah, Hal - le - lu - jah, Hal - le - lu - jah, Hal - le - lu - jah, Hal -
Hal - le - lu - jah, Hal - le - lu - jah, Hal - le - lu - jah, Hal - le - lu - jah, Hal -
Hal - le - lu - jah, Hal - le - lu - jah, Hal - le - lu - jah, Hal - le - lu - jah, Hal -
Hal - le - lu - jah, Hal - le - lu - jah, Hal - le - lu - jah, Hal - le - lu - jah, Hal -
8
142
159
172
A
- le - lu - jah! for the Lord God Om - ni - po - tent reign - eth, Hal - le -
- le - lu jah! for the Lord God Om - ni - po - tent reign - eth, Hal - le -
- le - lu - jah! for the Lord God Om - ni - po - tent reign - eth, Hal - le -
- le - lu - jah! for the Lord God Om - ni - po - tent reign - eth, Hal - le -
11
- lu - jah, Hal - le - lu - jah, Hal - le - lu - jah, Hal - le - lu - jah!
- lu - jah, Hal - le - lu - jah, Hal - le - lu - jah, Hal - le - lu - jah! for the Lord
- lu - jah, Hal - le - lu - jah, Hal - le - lu - jah, Hal - le - lu - jah! for the Lord
- lu - jah, Hal - le - lu - jah, Hal - le - lu - jah, Hal - le - lu - jah! for the Lord
15

Hal - le - lu - jah, Hal - le - lu - jah, Hal - le-
God Om - ni - po - tent reign - eth, Hal - le - lu - jah, Hal - le - lu - jah, Hal - le-
God Om-ni - po-tent reign-eth, Hal-le-lu-jah, Hal-le-lu-jah, Hal-le-
God Om - ni - po - tent reign - eth, Hal - le - lu - jah, Hal - le - lu - jah, Hal - le-
18
WS
EP
P
B
173
143
160
- lu - jah, Hal - le - lu - jah! for the Lord God Om - ni - po - tent
- lu - jah, Hal - le - lu - jah! Hal-le-
- lu-jah, Hal-le-lu-jah! Hal-le-lu-jah, Hal-le - lu-jah, Hal-le-lu-jah, Hal -
- lu - jah, Hal - le - lu - jah!
21
reign - eth, Hal - le - lu - jah, Hal - le - lu - jah, Hal - le - lu -
- lu - jah, Hal - le - lu - jah, Hal - le - lu - jah, Hal - le - lu - jah, Hal - le - lu -
- le - lu - jah, Hal-le-lu-jah! for the Lord
Hal - le - lu - jah! for the Lord
24

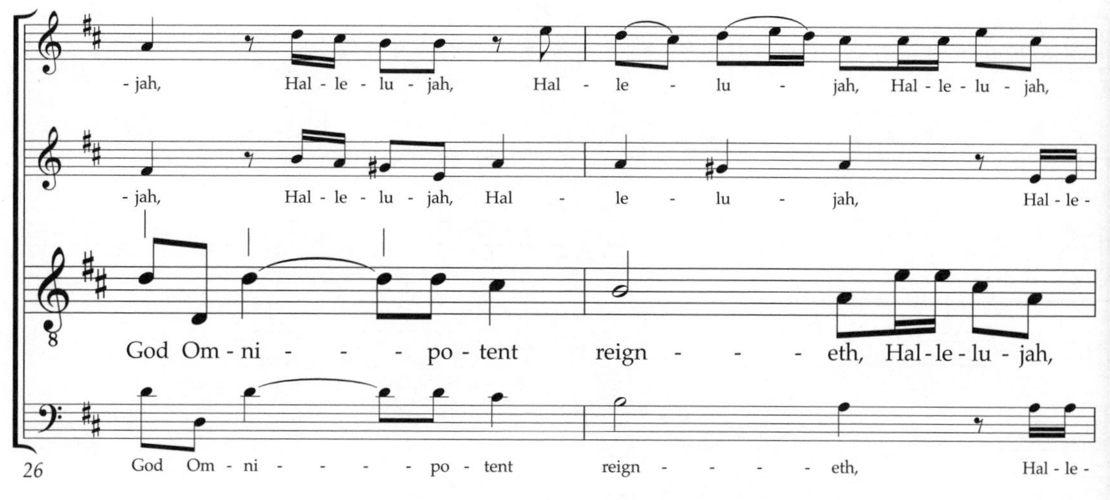
- jah, Hal - le - lu - jah, Hal - le - lu - jah, Hal - le - lu - jah,
- jah, Hal - le - lu - jah, Hal - le - lu - jah, Hal - le -
God Om - ni - - - po - tent reign - - - - eth, Hal - le - lu - jah,
God Om - ni - - - - po - tent reign - - - - eth, Hal - le -
26

Hal - le - lu - jah, Hal - le - lu - jah, Hal - le - lu - jah, Hal - le - lu - jah,
- lu - jah, Hal - le - lu - jah! for the Lord
Hal - le - lu - jah, Hal - le - lu - jah! for the Lord
- lu - jah, Hal - le - lu - jah, Hal - le - lu - jah, Hal - le -
28

174
Hal - le - lu - jah, Hal - le - lu - jah, Hal - le - lu - jah, Hal -
God Om - ni - - - po - tent reign - - - eth, Hal - le - lu - jah,
God Om - ni - - - po - tent reign - - - eth, Hal -
- lu - jah, Hal - le - lu - jah, Hal - le - lu - jah, Hal - le - lu - jah, Hal - le -
30

144
161
(poco meno mosso)
C
-le - lu - jah! The king - dom of this world
Hal - le - lu - jah! The king - dom of this world
-le - lu - jah! The king-dom of this world
- lu-jah, Hal-le - lu - jah! The king - dom of this world
32
is be - come the King - dom of our Lord and of His
is be - come the King - dom of our Lord and of His
is be - come the King-dom of our Lord and of His
is be - come the King - dom of our Lord and of His
36
D
(a tempo)
175
Christ, and of His Christ;
Christ, and of His Christ;
Christ, and of His Christ; and
Christ, and of His Christ; and He shall reign for ev - er and ev - er,
40

162
f
and He shall reign for ev - er and
He shall reign for ev - er and ev - er, and He shall reign for ev - er and
for ev-er and ev - er, and He shall reign, and He shall reign for ev-er, for
44
145
E
f
and He shall reign for ev - er and ev - - - er. King of
ev - er, for ev-er and ev-er, for ev - er and ev - er. King of
ev - er, and He shall reign_ for ev-er and ev-er,
=
ev-er, for ev-er, for ev-er and ev-er, for ev - er, for ev - er and ev - er,
48
176
163
Kings, and Lord of Lords,
Kings, and Lord of Lords,
-4
-4
for ev-er and ev-er, Hal-le-lu-jah, Hal-le - lu-jah! for ev-er and
for ev - er and ev - er, Hal - le - lu - jah, Hal - le - lu - jah! for ev - er and
52

King of Kings,
for ever and
ever, Hal-le-lu-jah, Hal-le-lu-jah!
for ev-er and
ev - er, Hal - le - lu - jah, Hal - le - lu - jah!
for ev - er and
56
146
177
and Lord of Lords,
ev - er, Hal - le - lu - jah, Hal - le - lu - jah!
for ev - er and
ev-er, Hal-le-lu-jah, Hal-le-lu-jah!
for ev-er and
59
164
King of Kings
ev - er, Hal - le - lu - jah, Hal - le - lu - jah!
for ev - er and
ev-er, Hal-le-lu-jah, Hal-le-lu-jah!
for ev-er and
62

F
(rit.)
(a tempo)
ff
and Lord of Lords, and Lord of
ev - er, Hal - le - lu - jah, Hal - le - lu - jah!
King of Kings, and Lord of
-4
ev-er, Hal-le-lu-jah, Hal-le - lu - jah!
King of Kings, and Lord of
ev - er, Hal - le - lu - jah, Hal - le - lu - jah!
King of Kings, and Lord of
65
178
f
Lords, and He shall reign, and
Lords, and He shall reign, and He shall
=
Lords, and He shall reign, and He shall reign,
Lords, and He shall reign for ev - er and ev - - - er,
69
147
He shall reign for ev - er and ev - er, for ev - er and
reign for ev - er and ev - er, King of Kings, for ev - er and
and He shall reign for ev - er and ev - er, King of Kings,
and He shall reign for ev - er and ev - er, King of Kings, for ev - er and
72

P
165
W S
179
ev-er, Hal-le-lu-jah, Hal-le-lu-jah! and He shall reign for ev-er, for
ev-er, and Lord of Lords, Hal-le-lu-jah, Hal-le-lu-jah! and He shall reign for
and Lord of Lords, and He shall reign for ev-er, for
76
ev-er, and Lord of Lords, Hal-le-lu-jah, Hal-le-lu-jah! and He shall reign for ev-er, for
G
ev-er and ev-er, King of Kings, and Lord of Lords, King of
ev-er and ev-er, King of Kings, and Lord of Lords, King of
ev-er and ev-er, King of Kings, and Lord of Lords, King of
80
ev-er and ev-er, King of Kings, and Lord of Lords, King of
E P
148
P
166
Kings, and Lord of Lords, and He shall reign for ev-er and ev-
Kings, and Lord of Lords, and He shall reign for ev-er and ev-
Kings, and Lord of Lords, and He shall reign for ev-er and ev-
84
Kings, and Lord of Lords, and He shall reign for ev-er, for ev-er and ev-

END OF PART II

PART III

45 Air – I Know That My Redeemer Liveth (Soprano)

I know that my Redeemer liveth
And that He shall stand at the latter day
Upon the earth.
And though worms destroy this body
Yet in my flesh shall I see God.

For now is Christ risen from the dead
The first-fruits of them that sleep.

46 Chorus – Since By Man Came Death

CD1 Track 20 CD2 Tracks 75-76

7

al - so the re - sur - rec - tion of the dead, by man came al - so the re - sur -
al - so the re - sur - rec - tion of the dead, by man came al - so the re - sur -
al - so the re - sur - rec - tion of the dead, by man came al - so the re - sur -
al - so the re - sur - rec - tion of the dead, by man came al - so the re - sur -
11

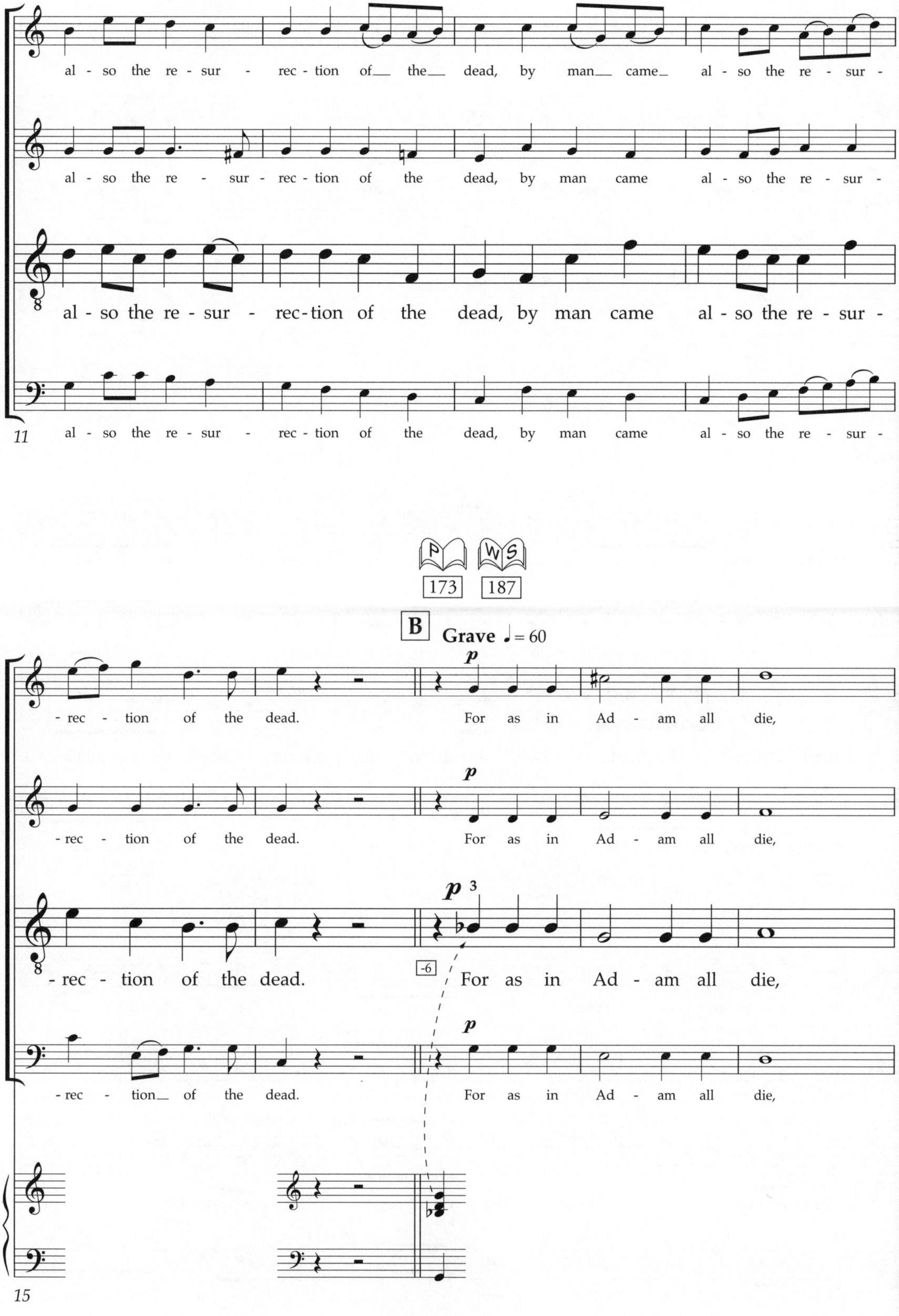

P 173 WS 187

B Grave ♩ = 60

p

- rec - tion of the dead. For as in Ad - am all die,

- rec - tion of the dead. For as in Ad - am all die,

- rec - tion of the dead. For as in Ad - am all die,

-6

- rec - tion of the dead. For as in Ad - am all die,

15

C
Allegro ♩ = 100
f
for as in Ad - am all die, e - ven so in
for as in Ad - am all die, e - ven so in
for as in Ad - am all die, e - ven so in
for as in Ad - am all die, e - ven so in
20
EP
155
Christ shall all be made a - live, e - ven so in Christ shall all be made a -
Christ shall all be made a - live, e - ven so in Christ shall all be made a -
Christ shall all be made a - live, e - ven so in Christ shall all be made a -
Christ shall all be made a - live, e - ven so in Christ shall all be made a -
24
P
174
WS
188
- live, e - ven so in Christ shall all, so in Christ shall
- live, e - ven so in Christ shall all, so in Christ shall
- live, e - ven so in Christ shall all, so in Christ shall
- live, e - ven so in Christ shall all, so in Christ shall
27

47 Recitative – Behold, I Tell You A Mystery (Bass)

Behold, I tell you a mystery
We shall not all sleep
But we shall all be changed in a moment
In the twinkling of an eye
At the last trumpet.

48 Air – The Trumpet Shall Sound (Bass)

The trumpet shall sound
And the dead shall be raised, incorruptible
And we shall be changed.

For this corruptible must put on incorruption
And this mortal must put on immortality.

49 Recitative – Then Shall Be Brought To Pass (Alto)

Then shall be brought to pass the saying that is written
Death is swallowed up in victory.

50 Duet – O Death, Where Is Thy Sting? (Alto & Tenor)

O death, where is thy sting?
O grave, where is thy victory?

The sting of death is sin
And the strength of sin is the law.

51 Chorus – But Thanks Be To God

Andante ♩= 92

But thanks, but thanks, thanks, thanks be to God, but thanks, but

But thanks, but thanks, thanks, thanks be to God, to God, thanks be to

+3

But thanks, but thanks, thanks, thanks be to God, thanks be to

But thanks, but thanks, thanks, thanks, be to God, thanks be to

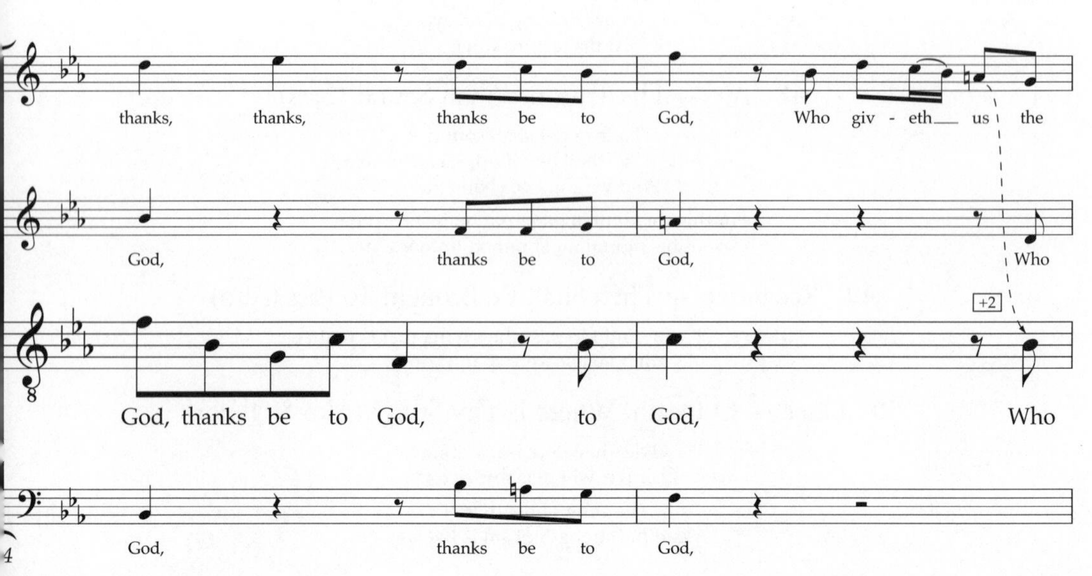

P 185
WS 200
vic - to - ry, the vic - to - ry through our Lord Je - sus
giv - eth us the vic - to - ry through our Lord Je - sus
giv - eth us the vic - to - ry through our Lord Je - sus
6

Christ,
Christ, Who giv - eth us the
Christ, Who giv - eth us the vic - to - ry, Who
+2
Who giv - eth us the vic - to - ry, the vic - to - ry through
8

Who giv - eth us the vic - to - ry through our Lord
vic - to - ry, Who giv - eth us the vic - to - ry through our Lord
giv - eth us, Who giv - eth us the vic - to - ry through our Lord
our Lord Je - - - sus Christ, through our Lord
10

165
A
Je - sus Christ,
Je - sus Christ, but thanks, but thanks, thanks be to God,
=
Je - sus Christ, but
Je - sus Christ,
12
186
201
but thanks, but thanks, but
thanks be to God,
thanks, but thanks, thanks, thanks be to God, to God,
but
15
thanks, but thanks, thanks be to God,
thanks be to God, but thanks, thanks be to
+2
thanks be to God, to God,
thanks, but thanks, but thanks be to God, thanks
17

thanks be to God, but thanks, but thanks, thanks,
God, to God, but thanks be to God,
-4
=
but thanks be to God, but
be to God, but thanks, but thanks, thanks be to God,
19
B
166
thanks, thanks be to God, thanks, thanks be to God, thanks be to
thanks, but thanks, thanks, thanks be to God, thanks be to God, to
22
187
202
God, Who
Who giv - eth us the vic - to - ry,
+3
God, Who giv - eth us the vic - to - ry,
25

C
27
giv - eth us the vic - to - ry, the vic - to - ry through our Lord
Who giv - eth us the vic - to - ry through our Lord
Who giv - eth us the vic - to - ry through our Lord
Who giv - eth us the vic - to - ry through our Lord
29
Je - sus Christ, but thanks be to God, but thanks, but thanks, thanks
Je - sus Christ, but thanks, thanks be to God, but thanks, but thanks,
Je - sus Christ, but thanks be to God, but thanks, but thanks,
Je - sus Christ, but thanks be to God, but thanks, but thanks,
P 188
WS 203
32
be to God, to God, Who giv - eth us the vic - to - ry, Who giv - eth us the
thanks be to God, Who
thanks be to God, Who giv - eth us the vic - to - ry, the
thanks be to God, Who giv - eth us the vic - to - ry, the

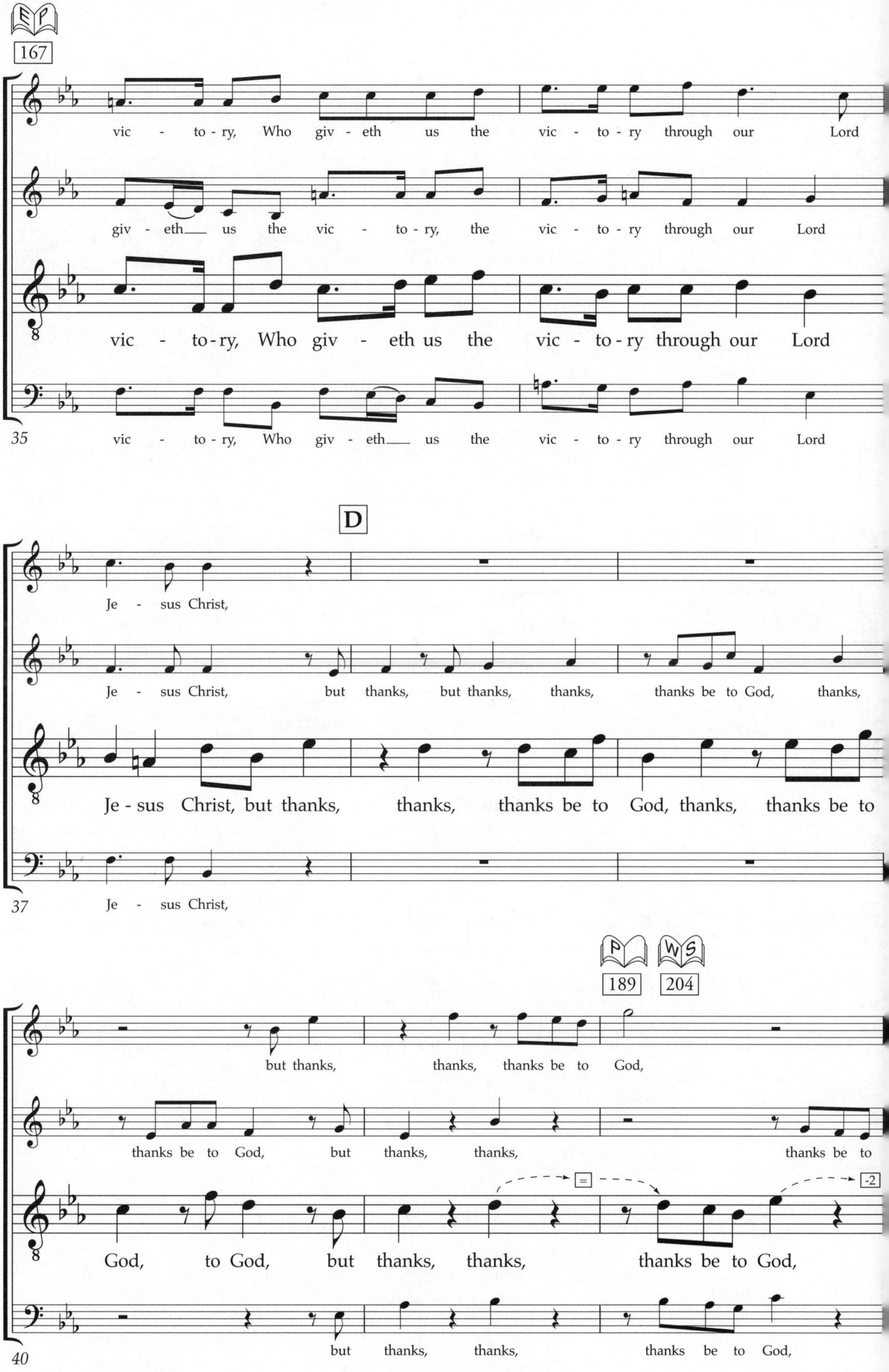

167

vic - to - ry, Who giv - eth us the vic - to - ry through our Lord

giv - eth us the vic - to - ry, the vic - to - ry through our Lord

vic - to - ry, Who giv - eth us the vic - to - ry through our Lord

35 vic - to - ry, Who giv - eth us the vic - to - ry through our Lord

D

Je - sus Christ,

Je - sus Christ, but thanks, but thanks, thanks, thanks be to God, thanks,

Je - sus Christ, but thanks, thanks, thanks be to God, thanks, thanks be to

37 Je - sus Christ,

52 Air – If God Be For Us, Who Can Be Against Us? (Soprano)

If God be for us, who can be against us?
Who shall lay anything to the charge of God's elect?

It is God that justifieth.
Who is he that condemneth?

It is Christ that died
Yea, rather that is risen again
Who is at the right hand of God
Who makes intercession for us.

53a Chorus – Worthy Is The Lamb That Was Slain

Largo ♩ = 60

f

S: Wor - thy is the Lamb that was slain, and hath re -

A: Wor - thy is the Lamb that was slain, and hath re -

T: Wor - thy is the Lamb that was slain, and hath re-

B: Wor - thy is the lamb that was slain, and hath re -

+3

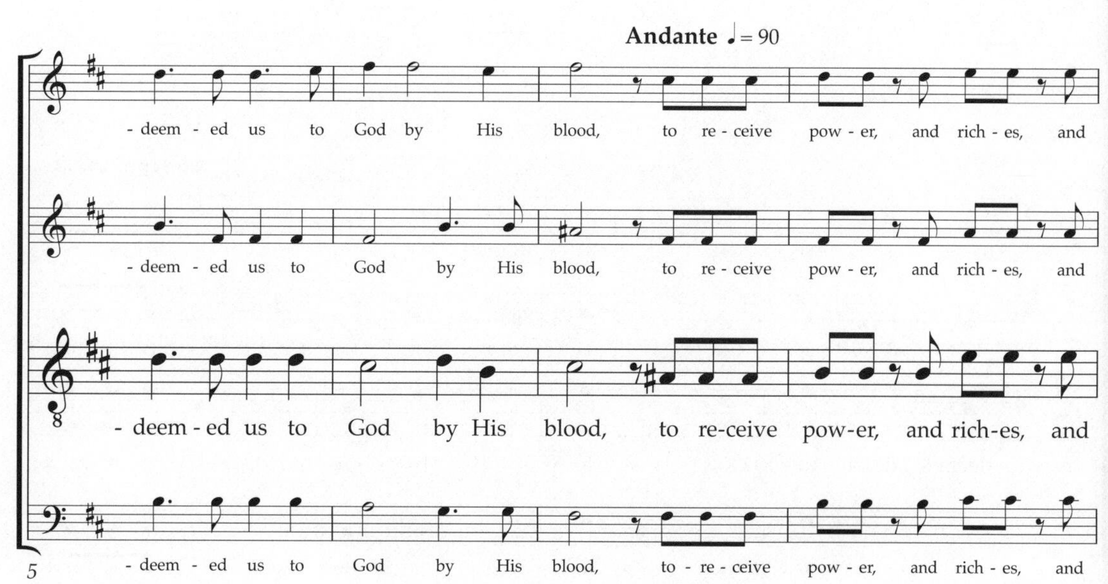

wis - dom, and strength, and hon - our, and glo - ry, and bless - ing.
wis - dom, and strength, and hon - our, and glo - ry, and bless - ing.
+3
wis-dom, and strength, and hon-our, and glo-ry, and bless-ing.
wis - dom, and strength, and hon - our, and glo - ry, and bless - ing.
9
WS
97
218
A
Largo ♩= 60
EP
174
Wor - thy is the Lamb that was slain, and hath re -
Wor - thy is the Lamb that was slain, and hath re -
Wor - thy is the Lamb that was slain, and hath re-
Wor - thy is the Lamb that was slain, and hath re -
12
Andante ♩= 90
- deem - ed us to God, to God by His blood, to re - ceive
- deem - ed us to God, to God by His blood, to re - ceive
- deem - ed us to God, to God by His blood, to re-ceive
- deem - ed us to God, to God by His blood, to re - ceive
16

pow-er, and rich-es, and wis-dom, and strength, and hon-our, and glo-ry, and
20
P 198
WS 219
B
Larghetto (slightly slower) ♩= 84
bless-ing.
-6
Bless-ing and hon-our, glo-ry and pow'r, be un-to Him, be un-to
23
EP 175
Bless-ing and hon-our, glo-ry and
Him that sit-teth up-on the throne, and un-to the Lamb,
26

pow'r, be un - to Him be un - to Him that sit - teth up - on the
that
29
throne, and un - to the Lamb,
Bless - - - ing and
sit - teth up - on the throne, and un - to the Lamb,
31
199
220
for ev - er and ev - er, for ev - er and ev - er, glo - - - - -
hon - our, glo - ry and pow'r, be un - to Him, be un - to Him,
for ev - er and ev - er, for ev - er and ev - er, for ev - er and
bless - ing and hon - our, glo - ry and
33

- - - - - - ry,
for ev - er and ev - er, for ev - er, that
ev - er, for ev - er and ev - - - - er,
35 pow'r, be un - to Him, be un - to Him that sit - teth up - on the
176
that sit - teth up - on the throne, and
sit - teth up - on the throne, up - on the throne, and
and
37 throne, up - on the throne, up - on the throne, and
200
221
C
un - - - to the Lamb. Bless - ing and
un - - - to the Lamb. Bless - ing and hon - our, glo - ry and
un - to the Lamb.
39 un - - - to the Lamb. Bless - ing and hon - our, glo - ry and pow'r, be un - to

hon - our, glo - ry and pow'r, be un - to Him, glo -
pow'r, be un - to Him, glo - - - ry be un - to Him
Bless - ing and hon - our, glo - ry and pow'r, be un - to
Him for ev - er,
41
- ry be un - to Him that
that sit - teth up - on the throne,
Him, and un - to the Lamb,
that sit - teth up - on the throne,
43
77
201
222
sit - teth up - on the throne, that sit - teth up - on the throne,
that sit - teth up - on the throne for
Bless - ing and
and un - - - - to the Lamb for
46

for ev - er and ev - - - - - er, and un -
ev - er and ev - - - - - er, and un -
hon - our, glo - ry and pow'r, be un - to Him. Bless - ing and hon - our, glo - ry and
ev - er and ev - - - - - er. Bless - ing and hon - our, glo - ry and
48
to the Lamb for ev - er. Bless - ing and hon - our, glo - ry and pow'r, be un - to
to the Lamb for ev - er. Bless - ing and hon - our, glo - ry and pow'r, be un - to
pow'r, be un - to Him for ev - er. Bless - ing and hon - our, glo - ry and pow'r, be un - to
pow'r, be un - to Him for ev - er.
50
P 202
WS 223
D
Him, be un - to Him,
ff
Him, be un - to Him, bless - ing and hon - our, glo - ry and pow'r, be un - to
ff
Him, be un - to Him, bless - ing and hon - our, glo - ry and pow'r, be un - to
ff
Bless - ing and hon - our, glo - ry and pow'r, be un - to
53

178
ff
bless - ing, hon - our, glo - ry and pow - er, be un - to
Him, be un - to Him, bless - ing, hon - our, glo - ry and pow - er, be un - to
Him, be un - to Him, bless - ing, hon - our, glo - ry and pow - er, be un - to
Him, be un - to Him, bless - ing, hon - our, glo - ry and pow - er, be un - to
55
Him that sit - teth up - on the throne, up - on the
Him that sit - teth up - on the throne,
Him that sit - teth up - on the
Him that sit - teth up - on the throne, and
58
203
224
E
throne, and un - to the Lamb, for ev - er, for
and un - to the Lamb, for ev - er, for ev - er, for ev - er, for
throne, and un - to the Lamb, for ev - er, for ev - er, for ev - er, for
un - to the Lamb, un - to the Lamb, for ev - er, for ev - er, for
60

179
ev - er and ev - er, for ev - er and ev - er, for
ev - er and ev - er, for ev - er and ev - er, for
+2
+2
ev - er and ev - er for ev - er and ev - er, for
ev - er and ev - er, for ev - er and ev - er, for
63

ev - er and ev - er, for ev - er and ev - er, for
ev - er and ev - er, for ev - er and ev - - - -
+2
ev - er and ev - er, for ev - er and ev - er, for
ev - - - er and ev - - - - er, for ev - - er and ev - - - -
65

Adagio
ev - er, for ev - er and ev - er, for ev - er and ev - - - - er.
- er, for ev - er and ev - er, for ev - er and ev - - - - er.
ev - er, for ev - er and ev - er, for ev - er and ev - er.
- er, for ev - er and ev - er, for ev - er and ev - - - - er.
67

P 9 | P 204 | WS 225

CD 1 Track 23

F

Allegro moderato ♩ = 104

f

72 A - - - - - men, A - - - - - - - - - - men, A - - - - - - -

EP 180

f

A - - - - - - men, A - - - - - - - - - men, A -

77 - - - - men, A - men, A - men, A - men,

f

A - - - - - - - men, A - - - - - - - - - -

- - - - - - - - men, A - men, A - men,

81 A - - men, A - men,

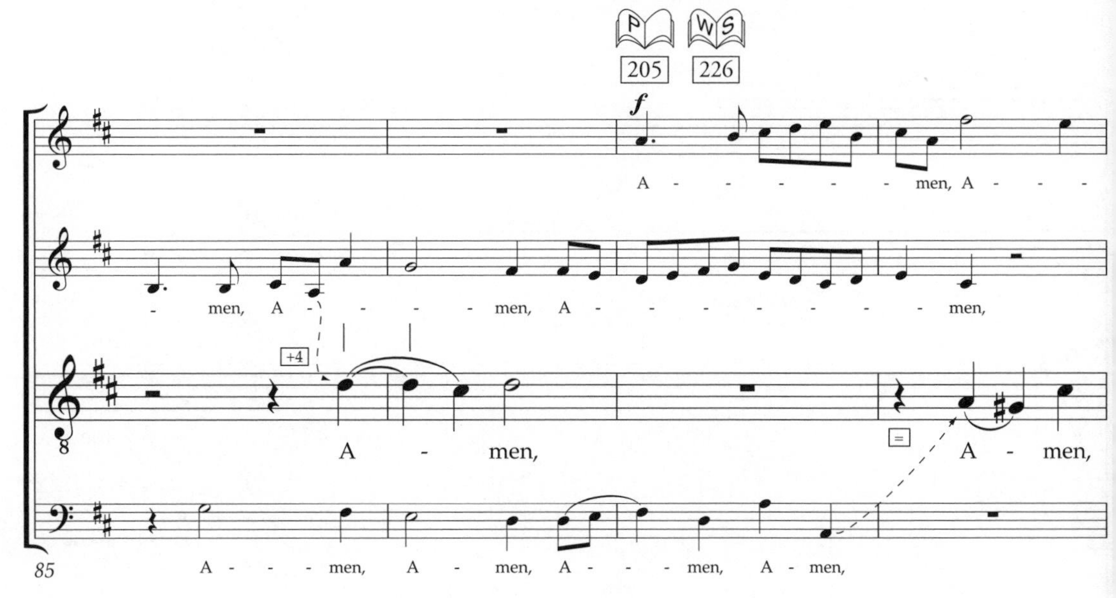

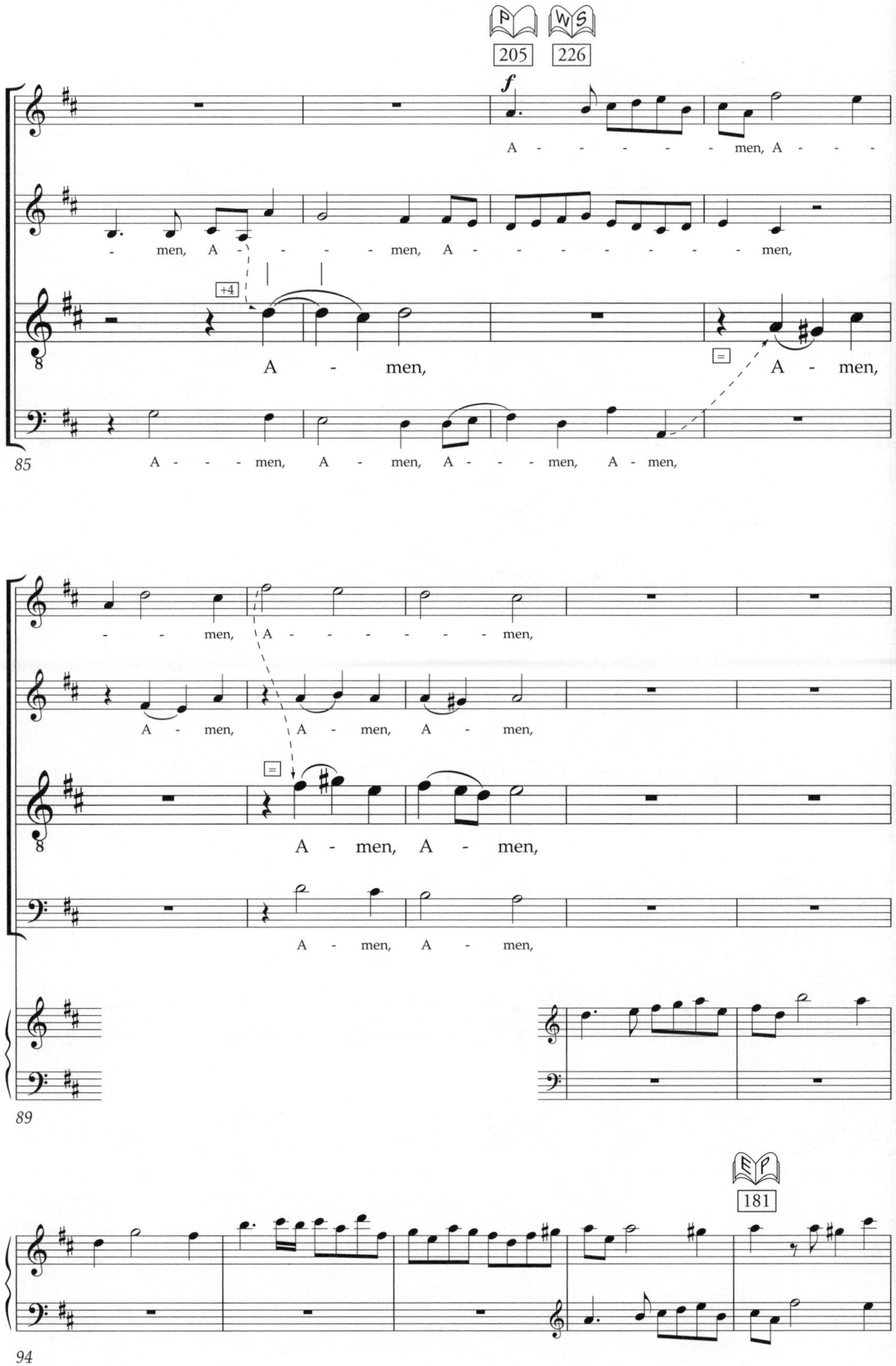

205
226
A - - - - - - men, A - - -
- men, A - - - - - men, A - - - - - - - - - - men,
+4
A - men,
=
A - men,
A - - - men, A - men, A - - - men, A - men,
85
- - men, A - - - - - - men,
A - men, A - men, A - men,
=
A - men, A - men,
A - men, A - men,
89
181
94

G
ff
A - - men,
ff
A - - men,
ff
A - men,
ff
A - - - -
99
206
227
A-men, A - men, A - - - - - - - - - - - men,
A-men, A - - - - - - - - - - - - - - - - men,
A - men, A - - - - - - - - men,
- men, A - - - - - - - men, A - - - - - men,
103

ff
A - - - men, A - men, A - - - - -
ff
A - - - - men, A - - - - - - - - men,
ff
+2
A - - - - men, A - - - - - men, A - men,
ff
A - - - - - - men, A - - - - - - - - - - - men, A -
108
EP
182
H
f
- men, A - - - - - - - - - - - - - - - men, A -
f
A - men, A - - - - - - - - - - - - - - - men,
f
+2
A - men, A - - - - - - - - - - - - - - men, A -
f
- - men, A - - - - - - - - - - - - - - men,
113
P
207
WS
228
- - - - - - - - - - - - - - - - - men,
A - - - - - - - - - - - men, A - - - - - - - - - -
- - - - - - - - - men, A - - - - men, A - - - -
A -
117

I
A - - - - - - men,
A -
- - - - - men, A - - - - - men, A - - - - - - - - -
- - - - - men,
A - - - - - - - - - -
121
- - - - - - - - men,
183
- - - - - - - men, A - men,
- - - - - - men, A - - - - - men, A - - - men,
- - - - - - - men, A - - - - - - - - - -
125
A - - - - - - men, A - - - - men, A - - - - - - - -
208
229
A - - - - - - - - - - - - - - - men,
A - - - - - - - - - - - - - - - - men,
- men, A - - - - - - - men, A - - -
129
- - men, A - - - - - - men, A - - - - - - - -

K
A - men, A - men,
A - men, A - men, A - men,
133
A - men, A - men, A - men,
137
184
L
209
230
men, A - men, A
141

145
ff
- - - - - - - - - - - - - - men, A -
ff
- - - - - - - - men, A - - - - men, A - - - - men, A -
ff
- - men, A - men, A - men, A - - - - - - -
ff
- - - - - - - - - men, A - - - - - - - - - - - - - - -
150
- - - - - men, A - - - - - - - - - men, A - - - -
- - - - - - men, A - - - - - - - - men, A - men,
- - - - men, A - men, A - men,
- - - - - men, A - - - - - - - men, A - - - men,
154
Adagio
- - - - - - men, A - men, A - - - men.
A - men, A - men, A - men, A - - - men.
-2
A - men, A - men, A - men, A - men.
G.P.
A - men, A - men, A - men, A - - - men.